RAND

Countywide Evaluation of the Long-Term Family Self-Sufficiency Plan

Countywide Evaluation Report

Elaine Reardon, Robert F. Schoeni, Lois M. Davis,
Jacob Alex Klerman, Jeanne Ringel,
John Hedderson, Paul S. Steinberg,
Sarah C. Remes, Laura Hickman, Eric Eide,
Marian Bussey, John Fluke

Prepared for the County of Los Angeles

RAND Labor & Population

The research described in this report was conducted by RAND Labor & Population
for the County of Los Angeles.

ISBN: 0-8330-3195-3

Published 2002 by RAND
1700 Main Street, P.O. Box 2138, Santa Monica, CA 90407-2138
1200 South Hayes Street, Arlington, VA 22202-5050
201 North Craig Street, Suite 202, Pittsburgh, PA 15213
RAND URL: http://www.rand.org/
To order RAND documents or to obtain additional information, contact Distribution
Services: Telephone: (310) 451-7002; Fax: (310) 451-6915; Email: order@rand.org

PREFACE

The Los Angeles County Board of Supervisors (the Board) adopted the Long-Term Family Self-Sufficiency (LTFSS) Plan on November 16, 1999. The LTFSS Plan consists of 46 projects with a unifying goal to promote self-sufficiency among families that are participating in the California Work Opportunity and Responsibility to Kids (CalWORKs) program, former CalWORKs families, and other low-income families. The Chief Administrative Office (CAO) is the lead agency responsible for implementing the evaluation of the LTFSS Plan. On December 5, 2000, the Board approved the implementation plan for the evaluation of the LTFSS Plan Project #46. Following an open and competitive bidding process, the Board awarded RAND a contract to conduct a Countywide Evaluation of the LTFSS Plan, and a subcontract was awarded to Walter R. McDonald and Associates (WRMA) to work jointly with RAND on the Evaluation.

The contract stipulated that one of the deliverables would be an annual Countywide Evaluation Report. This document constitutes the first of three such reports based on work performed through January 2002.

For more information about RAND's evaluation of the LTFSS Plan, contact:
Elaine Reardon
Project Director
Associate Economist
RAND
1700 Main Street
Santa Monica, CA 90407

CONTENTS

TABLES

FIGURES

EXECUTIVE SUMMARY

INTRODUCTION

The California Work Opportunity and Responsibility to Kids Act of 1997 (CalWORKs) provided Los Angeles County (hereafter, the County) with a large stream of funds. The County Board of Supervisors (hereafter, the Board) instructed the County's New Directions Task Force (NDTF) to develop a Long-Term Family Self-Sufficiency (LTFSS) Plan for CalWORKs recipients and the broader low-income population, with the purpose of selecting projects that would improve the capacity of families to become self-sufficient. Each of the projects was to: (1) have an adequate evaluation design to track achievement of measurable outcomes; (2) not duplicate existing services; (3) be culturally and linguistically sensitive; (4) not supplant existing funding; and (5) address a clearly documented need. To identify those projects and more broadly to guide the LTFSS effort, the NDTF adopted Mark Friedman's Results-Based Decision Making (RBDM) Framework (hereafter, the RBDM Framework). The NDTF effort resulted in the 46 projects known collectively as the LTFSS Plan that was approved by the Board on November 16, 1999.

The Chief Administrative Office (CAO) is the lead agency responsible for implementing the evaluation of the LTFSS Plan. The evaluation is taking place on two levels: the Countywide level and the individual projects level. The contract to evaluate outcomes at the county level was awarded to RAND by the Board after an open and competitive bidding process. In brief, this evaluation is not on the individual progress of 46 projects, but on the progress the County has made in achieving its goal of long-term family self-sufficiency. The contract stipulated that one deliverable would be an annual Countywide Evaluation Report. This document, which is the first of three such reports, draws from three previous RAND reports produced under the contract.

RESULTS AND OUTCOMES

The LTFSS Plan includes 46 projects working toward a single result: sustained self-sufficiency for CalWORKs families, former CalWORKs families, and other low-income families in Los Angeles County. In pursuit of this result, the NDTF identified 26 measurable indicators to evaluate progress toward achieving the Board's five outcomes for children and families—good health, safety and survival, economic well-being, social and emotional well-being, and educational and workforce readiness.

Because there are a large number of indicators, the County decided it would be helpful to identify one indicator for each outcome area to serve as a "headline" indicator. The analysis to determine the 5 headline indicators was based on the RBDM Framework's criteria—communication power, proxy power, and, in particular, data power. The headline indicators selected were: low birth weight births (good health); domestic violence arrests (safety and survival); annual income under poverty level (economic well-being); personal behaviors harmful to self/others, as measured by child abuse and neglect (social and emotional well-being); and teenage high school graduation (education and workforce readiness). In addition to the headline indicators, data will be collected and evaluated for another 12 indicators. Finally, 9 of the indicators have been placed on a Data Development Agenda.

BASELINE DATA AND THE STORY BEHIND THE BASELINES

Using the 17 indicators that were not placed on the Data Development Agenda and, in particular, the 5 headline indicators, RAND, following the approach laid out in the RBDM Framework, collected and analyzed the data over time to develop baselines for the indicators, stories behind the baselines to explain what factors influence the trends in the baselines, and forecasts of the likely future levels of the indicators.

For the first headline indicator—low birth weight births—the analysis shows that the percent of infants born weighing less than 2,500 grams has been increasing in the County during the 1990s, to around 6.3 percent in the year 2000. Of the possible explanations for this trend, the analysis shows that the increase can be attributed primarily to increases in the percentage of multiple births, which tend to have much lower birth weights than single births; the percentage of multiple births increased 25 percent during the 1990s.

For the second headline indicator—domestic violence arrests—the analysis shows that the domestic violence arrest rate—measured as the number of arrests per 100,000 population age 18 and over—grew in the County from 197.6 to 276.7 between 1988 and 1997, declining thereafter such that by 2000 it was

211.7. In this case, the observed increases can be viewed as an improvement because they appear to be driven by the increasing police use of arrest in domestic violence situations and efforts by many local organizations to address domestic violence, including improving police response. The cause of the decline since 1997 is unclear, although some nationwide evidence suggests that domestic violence incidents and, therefore perhaps arrests, are also declining.

For the third headline indicator—annual income under poverty level (defined as the percentage of people living in families whose income is below the federal poverty threshold)—the analysis shows a rapid decline since the mid-1990s, from 25 percent of Angelenos living in poverty in 1994 to 16 percent in 2000. Despite the substantial improvements since 1994, the long-run trend over the entire 25-year period for which data are available has been toward higher poverty. The long-run increase in poverty can be viewed in terms of the racial/ethnic composition of the population. Compared to 25 years ago, a higher percentage of Angelenos today are Hispanic, a racial/ethnic group with a high poverty rate. The short-run fluctuations in poverty result primarily from changes in the macroeconomy. Although the latest data are for 2000, we expect that poverty levels continued to fall in 2001, given that the economy in the County expanded during the past two years. In addition, some of the recent decline is likely associated with changes in welfare policy.

For the fourth headline indicator—personal behaviors harmful to self or others (measured by child abuse and neglect, which in turn is defined as the number of substantiated child abuse and neglect cases per 1,000 children in the population)—the analysis shows that, over the entire 1990s, child abuse and neglect declined in the County during the 1990s, but the decline was not continuous. Between 1990 and 1992, the rate fell from 32 to 23 per 1,000. However, this fall was followed by a substantial rise to 37 by 1996. After 1996, the rate declined in each of the subsequent four years, leaving the rate at 15 per 1,000, or one-half the level that existed at the beginning of the decade. The change in the rate of substantiated cases of child abuse and neglect may be the result of changes in reporting, changes in the response of child safety officials, and/or actual changes in the incidence of child abuse. Each of these factors is affected by public awareness of preventive efforts and community and environmental trends. The recession of the early to mid-1990s, which caused an increase in poverty and a rise in welfare participation, was most likely an important cause of the increase in the child abuse and neglect rate. It is likely to have increased parental stress and, in turn, child abuse. Similarly, the subsequent improvements in the labor market and poverty likely contributed to the decline in child abuse in the late 1990s.

For the fifth headline indicator—teenage high school graduation rate—the analysis shows the high school graduation rate was virtually unchanged at around 62 percent in the County during the period for which estimates are available, 1997–2000. Research suggests that the factors affecting high school completion include race/ethnicity, family background, labor market forces, and public policy.

For each headline indicator, this document provides a forecast of future outcomes had the LTFSS Plan not been implemented. The methods and factors influencing the forecasts differ across indicators. As the Plan is implemented, these forecasts can be compared to actual outcomes in the year 2001 and beyond to assess the success of the LTFSS Plan in improving the lives of low-income families.

THE PROJECTS AND THEIR PARTNERS

Of the 46 projects that comprise the Plan, how many target which outcomes and what effect are they having on those outcome areas? In terms of the first part of the question, 12 projects target good health; 10, safety and survival; 16, economic well-being; 11, social and emotional well-being; and 17, education and workforce readiness. Another 11 nondirect service projects support the achievement target of all outcome areas. As for the second part of the question, as of January 2002, only half the projects had begun delivering services to their clients, some of these only recently. Thus, it is too early to incorporate the results from project evaluations. Although many projects (and most of the implemented projects) have submitted their preliminary evaluation deliverables, none has completed its project evaluation report.

The holistic approach of the Plan implies that many partners are involved with helping the County achieve its goals, not just County agencies, though the process is predominantly led by County agencies. Lead agencies can provide services and may also play supporting roles to other projects, including:

- Serving as service providers for other projects;

- Co-locating staff with other departments or agencies as part of an LTFSS project or having staff that comprise part of multi-disciplinary teams;
- Having treatment providers who may be affected by other LTFSS projects (e.g., referrals will be made to these providers);
- Co-leading an LTFSS project with another lead agency; and
- Providing technical support to other projects (e.g., assistance with the development of monitoring tools).

The lead agencies and partners include the NDTF, the Department of Public Social Services (DPSS), the Department of Children and Family Services, the Department of Health Services, the Department of Mental Health, the Probation Department, the CAO/SIB, the Department of Human Resources, the Public Library, the Community Development Commission, the Los Angeles County Public Counsel, the Children's Planning Council, the County Sheriff's Department, the Los Angeles Police Department, the Los Angeles County Office of Education, the Los Angeles Unified School District, Workforce Investment Boards, Department of Labor Welfare-to-Work Grantees, Community Colleges, Adult Schools, Regional Occupational Centers, Job Club contractors, SEIU 660, Medi-Cal 1931(b) outreach contractors, the Metropolitan Transit Authority, domestic violence service providers, the National Family Life and Education Center, CalLEARN contractors, child care resource and referral agencies, and other community-based organizations (CBOs).

In our interviews, several lead agencies commented that working with the LTFSS Plan target population is new to their departments. Their LTFSS projects have enabled them to begin developing new relationships with the community (as well as with other County agencies). These cooperative alliances are among the changes that the Plan was designed to accomplish.

ASSESSMENT OF THE LTFSS PLAN AND RBDM FRAMEWORK

The LTFSS Plan has three stages: planning, implementation, and evaluation. The RBDM Framework is a planning and evaluation tool that emphasizes collaboration and partnerships; however, it does not provide specific guidance on implementation. Thus, we discuss our assessment of implementation of the LTFSS Plan in terms of the goal of the Plan, rather than in terms of the effectiveness of the RBDM Framework.

How useful was the RBDM Framework in conducting the planning process for the plan? Based on interviews with key informants, the RBDM Framework succeeded in focusing attention on ultimate results. In particular, the RBDM Framework helped planners focus on the result(s) or outcome(s) they wanted to improve and identify a list of outcome indicators that quantify the achievement of the outcomes; then, it urges planners to choose strategies that they believe will improve those outcomes. Further, the RBDM Framework urges planners to involve all the relevant stakeholders in a collaborative process to decide which result(s) to achieve or outcome(s) to influence and to select indicators to measure progress toward this goal.

The interviews also suggested that a longer planning process would have made it easier to apply the RBDM Framework. The RBDM Framework does not specify a time frame over which planning should be accomplished but stresses that planning is an iterative process, in which results feed back into additional planning and efforts to refine the overall program and its component projects. The County used its previous experience planning welfare reform as a guide, allowing six months for overall planning, including eight weeks for developing proposals. Looking back on their experiences with the LTFSS Plan, many interviewees thought that in future applications of the RBDM Framework, the planning and project selection process would benefit from more time. They felt this would lead to a number of improvements: even wider community participation in planning, more discussion of how the projects fit together and how they fit into the County's existing service-delivery system, and more thorough discussion of all possible options for spending the funds.

How did the LTFSS Plan as a whole affect the implementation of the individual projects and the delivery of services to the County's low-income population? Our interviews suggested that the LTFSS Plan has slowed project implementation and the delivery of services. The initial budgets for the projects had constant funding through the five budget years, implicitly assuming that projects would be providing services at their steady-state level early in the first year (i.e., soon after July 2000). The reality has been quite different. Initial Board approval for the LTFSS Plan as a whole had been conditional on the Board's subsequent review and approval of the Implementation Plan of projects using Performance Incentive Funds (PIF). Projects could not begin spending funds or providing services until the second Board approval was received. For tracking purposes, the official DPSS *LTFSS Project Status Update* breaks the LTFSS Plan's 46 projects into 59 units (some projects are tracked at the subproject level; e.g., when lead responsibility for parts of the project are assigned to different departments). For these 59 units, the April 2002 Status Update provides current details. Of them, 23 did not require Board approval, 18 were pending Board approval, and 18 had been approved (6 before July 2000, 10 between July 2000 and June 2001, and 2 since then). Similarly, 29 projects are officially listed as not having begun providing services, with the remaining 39 providing services (3 starting before July 2000, 15 between July 2000 and June 2001, and 11 since July 2001). Even this figure for beginning to provide services sometimes provides an overly positive impression of the status of project rollout. Official Year-to-Date Expenditures as of February 28, 2002, imply that of the 38 non-DPSS projects (using an assignment of projects to departments slightly different than in the Project Status Update) only 7 spent any funds in the first year (July 2000 to June 2001) and only 2 more projects have spent any funds in the current year (i.e., through the reporting date, though there is reason to believe that expenditure reports are incomplete).

Some of this slow project rollout is a small project phenomenon. Fourteen of the 59 projects have total budgets of at least $2.5 million. Of them, 7 were delivering services by July 1, 2001. Of the remaining 7, 3 began delivering services since then; leaving only 4 (28 percent) that have not yet delivered services. In contrast, of the 45 projects with total budgets of less than $2.5 million, only 19 have begun services, leaving 26 (59 percent) that have yet to begin delivering services.

This slow project rollout appears to have multiple causes. Part of the reason appears to be conventional problems with beginning new projects or, to a lesser extent, expanding existing projects—acquiring space, issuing RFPs and awarding contracts, negotiating interdepartmental and interagency memoranda of understanding, hiring staff, and providing training. Given county procedures, these processes often take six months or more.

An additional reason, directly related to the LTFSS Plan structure, appears to be the multiple approvals required before projects could proceed—coordination between the lead County agency and DPSS and then approval by the Board. Because PIF flow through DPSS and are required to satisfy the regulations of the funding agency, the California Department of Social Services, DPSS required lead County agencies using PIF to clear their budgets and plans with DPSS. It appears to have taken DPSS about a year to provide guidance to lead County agencies about the coordination process and to put that coordination process into place. In addition, despite the fact that, for projects funded with PIF, funds could not be spent until the Board approved the Implementation Plan, developing those plans required considerable senior staff time—for which new funds, and therefore new positions, were not yet available. In addition, this review process combined with DPSS leadership of the NDTF caused some projects to view the LTFSS Plan as a DPSS effort, and that view appears to have influenced department buy-in.

In some cases, the LTFSS Plan's service-integration strategy appears to have contributed to slow project rollout. Truly integrated service delivery requires close coordination between multiple departments in developing procedures and funding. Such integration requires more up-front planning, which takes time. In some cases, problems reaching consensus on choices further slowed project rollout.

Even together, it does not appear that these reasons are a complete explanation for slow project rollout. Our interviews with participants in the process suggested variation in the priority assigned to the LTFSS projects on the part of the lead County agencies. LTFSS Coordinators in some departments reported that they had trouble getting the attention of senior department staff or gaining sufficient resources to plan and implement their LTFSS projects.

The reason for this variation in priority given to LTFSS projects is unclear. In some cases, it appears that lead County agencies and project staff felt that the projects had been forced on them by outsiders involved in the open LTFSS planning process. In some cases, this resulted in their disagreeing with the basic program model or feeling that equivalent programs already existed. In some cases, lead County agencies were simply busy with a host of other tasks. As noted above, in the short-term, no additional staff was available. The slower rollout of smaller projects suggests that for some departments, the LTFSS projects may not have been large enough to warrant the management attention required to overcome the administrative hurdles. Finally, at least three departments—including DPSS—were undergoing major reorganizations during this period that also affected, for example, staffing of LTFSS projects. Rolling-out LTFSS Plan projects simply had to compete with other priorities and the steps leading to project rollout were repeatedly pushed off of the active agenda for a variety of reasons.

Beyond issues of speed of rollout, our interviews revealed two issues that resulted because the Plan was not articulated precisely enough to implement. First, although the framework was developed and shared, the Plan lacked interdepartmental procedures to facilitate contractual, financial, and project administration issues between departments. Second, it assumed that implementers would fulfill planner's conceptualized projects. By the County's charter and by its practices, the County has a strong Board, no elected executive, and departments that report directly to the Board. This structure implies that interdepartmental operations are negotiations between equals. A consequence of this structure is that multi-agency initiatives must be carefully planned, including all relevant department staff, to ensure that each entity's regulations are upheld. Furthermore, these additional coordination steps are likely to slow project rollout. Finally, while the Board made the NDTF the lead on the LTFSS Plan, in practice, the LTFSS Plan was often perceived as a DPSS effort. This perception appears to have limited the buy-in and efforts of some departments and has thereby slowed project rollout.

In addition, our interviews showed that the LTFSS Plan needs more formal links between planning and implementation. In a county the size of Los Angeles County, those responsible for planning often differ from those implementing an initiative. This leaves room for differences in interpretation of the vision laid forth by the planners and the possibility of developing programs that may not be feasible or represent the best use of agency resources. Similarly, because the Plan lacks a mechanism for having implementers' input heard by planners, there is a risk that implementers will not be as invested in the product as the planners.

ASSESSMENT OF EVALUATION FRAMEWORK

Evaluation is a key component of the RBDM Framework because it focuses on reported results, which are then used to guide future programmatic, fiscal, and operational decisions. An adequate evaluation design to track achievement of the five outcomes is also one of the five mandatory elements of the Plan. Our interviews revealed that the LTFSS Plan Evaluation Design helped introduce lead agency staff to the RBDM Framework, and a number of participants praised Friedman's model and its utility in terms of helping individuals at all levels to focus on client-level outcomes versus simple organizational process measures, such as how many people were served.

Interviewee comments suggested that while the RBDM Framework used in the LTFSS Plan Evaluation Design is accepted as a useful guide to planning an evaluation, there is some ambivalence about it in practice (i.e., in evaluating how successful projects are in affecting certain outcomes and using this information to guide future decisionmaking). We identified three sources for this ambivalence: confusion about how to conduct evaluations and how to apply the RBDM Framework, disagreement with the evaluation methodology, and project resistance to having their programs evaluated. The majority of those interviewed were concerned with how to conduct evaluations and how to implement the RBDM Framework, and a third of those interviewed directly disagreed with the evaluation methodology specified by the CAO.

Both the Evaluation Design Workgroup and the project-level interviewees mentioned difficulties in applying the RBDM Framework, including difficulty articulating the theoretical basis underlying the project effort, confusion about how to conceptualize and operationalize performance measures, and lack of guidance as to how to construct forecasts against which to measure actual progress. In terms of methodology, interviewees also commented that they thought the way a number of LTFSS projects were currently designed would make it impossible to evaluate their impact. Finally, several interviewees noted that there was some ambivalence by the lead agencies about the value of the evaluation process itself. With time, these fears may ease as comfort levels rise with familiarity.

QUALITY IMPROVEMENT STEPS

As of January 2002, almost three years after the initiation of the planning process and two years after the approval of the LTFSS Plan, about half the projects have begun to serve clients. This schedule is slower than had been expected, but in retrospect, implementation has proceeded about as fast as should have been expected. As experience accumulates, refined procedures and processes should allow for improved Plan performance.

Thus, this is an appropriate time for the NDTF to consider what progress the Plan has made toward achieving its goal. Moreover, the County's financial picture has changed, bringing with it a reassessment of its spending, including the LTFSS Plan. The Plan was conceived and executed at a time when there was considerable funding for the effort. By January 2002, however, the State's and County's financial situations had changed because of the economic recession and declining business investment, especially in technology. In light of this budgetary environment, we present an issue for the NDTF to consider to bring about more progress in relation to the baseline indicators.

The first issue concerns budgets. As the implementation of the LTFSS Plan moves into its third calendar year, lead agencies and LTFSS projects enter a new phase. From a management perspective, lead agencies will move from an emphasis on developing projects' implementation plans and putting an initial program in place to an emphasis on service delivery, refining LTFSS projects, overseeing contractors, and evaluating these projects and tracking outcomes. According to the RBDM Framework, the process is iterative. We are now well into the first cycle of planning, implementation, and evaluation. Lessons learned from implementation and evaluation should then cycle back into a follow-on planning phase. Based on those lessons, the RBDM Framework indicates that some projects would have their funding increased, some projects would have their funding decreased, some projects would be terminated, and some new projects would be initiated based on new or newly perceived needs and new program models developed elsewhere.

Successful and fast implementation contributes to a case for continued and perhaps increased funding. Similarly, RBDM Framework-based evaluation evidence of effectiveness should also contribute to a case for continued and perhaps increased funding. Finally, conventional research evidence of program efficacy and cost-effectiveness should also contribute to a case for continued and perhaps increased funding. Conversely, programs that had poor RBDM Framework-based evaluation outcomes, rolled out slowly, and had limited or negative research evidence from elsewhere should be at a higher risk of lower funding or even termination. Projects that have not yet implemented may have more difficult program models, but slow rollout may also be evidence of low buy-in from the lead agency, which does not bode well for the project's long-term prospects.

CLOSING THOUGHTS

The changed operating philosophy embodied in the LTFSS Plan itself has begun to stimulate real cultural change in the County and the lead agencies. In addition, the County and the projects have worked hard over the first two years of implementation to put procedures and infrastructure in place to deliver services to low-income families in the County. Nevertheless, many of the projects are not yet providing services or have only recently begun to do so. Over the next year, lead agencies have an opportunity to show that they can begin to provide services and that their programs can contribute to the well-being of these families and can positively affect the outcomes of interest.

ACKNOWLEDGMENTS

This report has greatly benefited from the contributions of a number of individuals. We wish to acknowledge the participants in the Countywide planning process, lead agency staff, and non-County representatives who willingly shared their experiences in planning and implementing the LTFSS Plan. We would like to express our thanks to those who provided us with access to planning documents, expenditure data, and the quantitative data we use to track county outcomes. We also wish to thank the LTFSS project coordinators, the Long-Term Family Self-Sufficiency Division and Financial Management Division, DPSS, and CAO/SIB staff.

Finally, we wish to express our appreciation to Amy Cox for her thoughtful review and comments on the draft report. Christopher Dirks provided valuable assistance in preparing this report.

ACRONYMS

AFDC	Aid to Families with Dependent Children
AHS	American Housing Survey
CalWORKs	California Work Opportunity and Responsibility to Kids Act of 1997
CAO	Chief Administrative Office
CAO/SIB	Chief Administrative Office/Services Integration Branch
CBO	Community-based organization
CDC	Community Development Commission
CDE	California Department of Education
CDF	California Department of Finance
CDJ	California Department of Justice
CDSS	California Department of Social Services
CPC	Children's Planning Council
CPS	Current Population Survey
CSS	Community and Senior Services
CTNA	CalWORKs Transportation Needs Assessment Survey
DCFS	Department of Children and Family Services
DHS	Department of Health Services
DMH	Department of Mental Health
DPSS	Department of Public Social Services
FPSI	Fiscal Policy Studies Institute
FY	fiscal Year
GAIN	Greater Avenues for Independence
GED	General Education Degree
JTPA	Job Training Partnership Act
LACOE	Los Angeles County Office of Education
LACHS	Los Angeles County Health Survey
LAC PROB	Los Angeles County Probation Department
LAPD	Los Angeles Police Department
LAUSD	Los Angeles Unified School District
LTFSS	Long-Term Family Self-Sufficiency
MDRC	Manpower Demonstration Research Corporation

MEDS	Medi-Cal Eligibility Determination System
MOU	Memorandum of understanding
NCVS	National Crime Victimization Survey
NDTF	New Directions Task Force
NDY	New Directions for Youth
PHN	Public Health Nurses
PIF	Performance Incentive Funds
ORG	Outgoing Rotation Group of the CPS
RBDM Framework	Mark Friedman's Results-Based Decision Making Framework
RFP	Request for Proposals
ROP	Regional Occupational Program
SD	Supervisorial district
SPA	Service Planning Area
STOP	Support and Therapeutic Options
TANF	Temporary Assistance for Needy Families
WIC	Woman, Infants, Children Program
WRMA	Walter R. McDonald and Associates
WTW	Welfare-to-Work

1. INTRODUCTION

BACKGROUND

The California Work Opportunity and Responsibility to Kids Act of 1997 (CalWORKs) provided Los Angeles County (hereafter, the County) with considerable new funding for social services. A combination of federal funding through block grants with a State Maintenance of Effort requirement and rapid caseload decline resulted in generous funding for State and County welfare operations. The CalWORKs legislation also provided that all the savings resulting from any decline in aid payments were to be returned to the counties in the form of "Performance Incentive Payments." The robust economy and the rapidly dropping caseload led to the accumulation of such PIF monies well in excess of any initial expectation. By early 1999, the County had "earned" about $400 million in PIF monies (later raised to about $460 million).

Rather than allocate all the funds to a single department, the Board of Supervisors (hereafter, the Board) used this opportunity to develop a unified plan to stabilize families "by building their capacity to become self-sustaining" (Board Minutes, April 13, 1999). At the Board's direction, the County's New Directions Task Force (NDTF) implemented a process to develop such a plan.

Specifically, the NDTF adopted Mark Friedman's Results-Based Decision Making Framework (hereafter, the RBDM Framework) to organize their planning (Friedman, 2001). The RBDM Framework led the County to begin by identifying the outcome area(s) it wanted to improve, the means by which it would measure progress toward the outcomes, and only then consider which projects and services would contribute toward achieving the desired results. The NDTF effort resulted in 46 projects known collectively as the Long Term Family Self-Sufficiency (LTFSS) Plan that was approved by the Board in November 1999. The final Plan formally expresses its vision with the following common themes:

- "Where possible, services to families should support the family as a unit, rather than focusing on individual family members in isolation.

- Just as individuals live in families, families live in communities. Therefore, strengthening communities is an important element of strengthening families.
- Services are most effective when integrated at a community level.
- Focusing on positive outcomes for families is key to delivering effective services."

Since the Plan's adoption, County agencies have moved to provide the services specified for the individual projects. Some projects are still in the planning stage; as of January 2002, about half have begun providing services.

In developing and implementing the Plan, the NDTF and the Workgroups that created the LTFSS Plan were explicitly guided by the RBDM Framework. The use of the RBDM Framework had three important implications for the development of the Plan. First, the RBDM Framework urges a focus not just on how well agencies and projects perform but on population-level results (i.e., the well-being of children, families, and communities). Consistent with this focus on population-level results, the LTFSS Plan projects were designed to address a set of key results and outcomes, discussed below.

Second, the RBDM Framework urges an open process, emphasizing the importance of opening deliberations from narrow department and agency discussions to the broader community. It does so both because broad community involvement leads to decisions that better reflect the preferences of the population and because having an impact on indicators of well-being is viewed as a collaborative process between government, community-based organizations (CBOs), and individual citizens.

Third, the RBDM Framework focuses on accountability. Projects are to track project-level performance measures, and the results of this tracking are expected to guide future project funding decisions. In addition, Countywide indicators of population-level outcomes are measured, and this information should also feed back into the Board's decisions about how available funds should be allocated.

OBJECTIVE

One of the projects funded by the LTFSS Plan—Project 46—was an evaluation to measure "the effectiveness of the Plan and various projects and services ... both to track progress and to guide future programmatic, fiscal, and operational decisions." The LTFSS Evaluation Design, in line with the RBDM Framework, employs two levels of evaluation. The first level is an overall assessment of the County's progress toward the result of self-sufficiency. As such, it is an evaluation of outcomes at the county population level. The second level of the evaluation includes each of the LTFSS projects, identifying and measuring progress on program performance measures. The first level, or Countywide Evaluation, is being performed under contract by RAND for the County, and has two parts: (1) an analysis of the LTFSS Plan Framework and Evaluation Framework, and (2) analyses of Countywide data on results and outcomes. Results from the first analysis are documented in an earlier report: *The LTFSS Plan Countywide Evaluation: Assessing the Utility of the LTFSS Plan Service Delivery and Planning Framework* (Davis et al., 2001); results from the second analysis are documented in two earlier reports: *The LTFSS Plan Countywide Evaluation: Indicators, Data Sources, and Geographical Analysis* (Hedderson and Schoeni, 2001) and *The LTFSS Plan Countywide Evaluation: Establishing the Baselines* (Schoeni et al., 2001).

One of the deliverables from the Countywide Evaluation is an annual Countywide Evaluation Report. This report, which is the first of three annual Countywide Evaluation Reports, draws from the earlier documents.

ORGANIZATION OF THIS REPORT

The structure of this report is driven by the outline provided in the LTFSS Plan Contract. Chapter 1—What's At Stake—briefly summarizes the importance of self-sufficiency and the five related outcomes. Chapter 3—Results and Outcomes—discusses the overall intended result in terms of the five outcome areas, the 26 indicators within those areas, and the five headline indicators selected (one from within each outcome area).

Chapter 4—Baseline Data and the Story Behind the Baselines—presents baseline trend data on the five headline indicators, explaining the causes and forces at work affecting those trends, forecasting the trends into the future, and measuring Countywide progress toward helping families achieve long-term self-sufficiency. Chapter 5—The Projects and Their Partners—describes the projects that are thought to affect each of the headline indicators and identifies the public and private partnerships associated with each project. Chapter 6—Assessment of the LTFSS Plan Framework—discusses the planning and service-delivery approach taken by the LTFSS Plan. Chapter 7—Assessment of the Evaluation Framework—reports on the utility of the evaluation framework and proposed amendments to it.

Finally, Chapter 8—Quality Improvement Steps—concludes this report, with suggested quality improvement steps for the NDTF to consider to further improve outcomes.

We also include two appendices. Appendix A lists the data sources underlying the analysis of the project indicators. Appendix B provides the data for the secondary (not headline) indicators. In future years, the appendix will also contain project evaluation reports.

2. WHAT'S AT STAKE

The ultimate goal of the LTFSS Plan is long-term self-sufficiency among low-income families in Los Angeles. In keeping with the transformation of welfare policy (Temporary Assistance for Needy Families [TANF] and CalWORKs) to requiring temporary assistance and the TANF/CalWORKs-based funding for the Plan, a narrow view of self-sufficiency might focus only on economic self-sufficiency. By this definition, families would be self-reliant if they did not depend on the government for monetary, health, or other forms of support. This narrow definition is related to two of the five outcomes the LTFSS Plan is designed to achieve: economic well-being; and education and workforce readiness. (See Chapter 3.)

However, economic well-being, as opposed to economic self-sufficiency, implies that families are doing better than simply not relying on government aid. In fact, the County chose three additional outcomes—good health, safety and survival, and social and emotional well-being—which, together with economic well-being and education and workforce readiness, point toward a broader agenda for children and families. As a whole, the five outcomes speak to a more generous vision of family self-sufficiency, one that promotes stable families and a nurturing environment for children.

The benefits of improving these outcomes are twofold. First, there is the savings achieved by reducing bad outcomes. For example, in the good health outcome area, children born with a low birth weight are known to face a higher risk of health and developmental problems throughout their childhood. These problems can be very costly, both for the family and for the community. An increased need for medical care across the life span represents the most significant cost associated with low birth weight. As evidence, one study has calculated that the incremental cost of low birth weight was $5.4 billion per year nationally in 1988 ($5.9 billion in 2000 dollars), with more than 75 percent of these costs attributed to medical care (Lewit et al., 1995). The remainder of the costs includes special education costs, costs of grade repetition, and child care costs. These estimates, however, do not include the costs of relatively rare but extremely costly needs, such as long-term care or institutionalization; thus, they may represent a lower bound. In Chapter 4, we show that the rate of low birth weight babies in Los Angeles County is rising. These dollar estimates suggest that if rates are not reduced, significant additional monetary costs will accrue to the County beyond simply the cost of the program.

Similarly, the LTFSS Plan seeks to increase public safety and survival, in part by decreasing the number of domestic violence incidents. (There are other mechanisms as well, such as providing safe places for children after school and placing Juvenile Probation Officers on school campuses.) In addition to the obvious human costs associated with domestic violence, there are significant monetary costs. These costs include medical and mental health care, temporary housing, and other social services. Consequently, reducing the incidence of domestic violence below the level that might occur in the absence of the LTFSS not only improves public safety but also could reduce costs. This is also the case for the social and emotional well-being outcome area: The monetary costs associated with child abuse and neglect, for example, include medical and mental health care, foster care, and other social services. Consequently, reducing the incidence of child abuse and neglect both improves public safety and may reduce costs.

In terms of economic well-being, an increase in the County's poverty rate will, all else equal, likely lead to increased expenditures on social services as more families become eligible for services and also have greater needs. At the same time, tax revenues will, all else equal, fall, since fewer people are working and have less disposable income to spend. As a result, the County may incur significant costs when the poverty rate increases. The same is true of homelessness: An increase in homelessness could raise the County's costs. According to a 1996 study of homelessness nationwide, homeless families with children reported an income only 46 percent as high as the poverty line (Burt et al., 1999). Homeless families also reported high levels of hunger, crime victimization, unemployment, and health problems. Treatment of these myriad problems could raise County costs unless successful interventions can reduce the incidence of homelessness.

Education is an important contributor to economic well-being, and education and workforce readiness is another outcome area targeted by the LTFSS Plan. People without a high school diploma (or General Education Degree, GED) are typically limited to low-wage jobs and are, thus, more vulnerable to economic downturns. This leads to greater hardship for the individual and potentially greater costs for the community. Because of the limited job market available to people who have not completed a high school degree, they are more likely to need social services, such as housing assistance or job training programs. In addition, low-wage jobs often do not provide fringe benefits, such as health insurance, and, thus, public hospitals and clinics may be the primary source of health care for these workers and their families. Without improvements in the education and workforce readiness of teenagers, for example, the relatively constant trend in the teenage high school graduation rate (which we discuss in Chapter 4) implies that the County would continue to pay the associated costs of low education levels and untrained residents.

That said, there is a second benefit to improving these outcomes through such efforts as the LTFSS Plan. We discussed some of the monetary costs associated with several of the bad outcomes targeted by the LTFSS Plan. Yet there are human costs as well, which while difficult to quantify, are equally important. There are personal, nonmonetary costs associated with domestic violence, child abuse, and the unexploited potential of families that are tragic, above and beyond their dollar cost to society.

Another way to think about this is to consider some of the families the LTFSS Plan projects have helped. Success stories cannot take the place of hard data on project outcomes, which is why the 45 projects (all but the evaluation project itself) have been charged with producing an evaluation of their impact, but the stories can give a concrete sense of the kinds of problems facing low-income families and how projects are trying to help them. Several projects replied to our request for more information about their clients, and we reproduce two of their success stories below.

PROJECT 34A: THE NURSE-FAMILY PARTNERSHIP PROGRAM[1]
"There are 25 public health nurses (PHN) working in the Nurse-Family Partnership throughout the County to support first-time pregnant young mothers by using this highly researched nurse home visitation model. The public health nurses help the mothers with all aspects of their life, such as assisting the mother in how to care for herself and her baby, apply for a job, and improve

___
[1]Memo from Kathye Petters-Armitage, Department of Health Services, December 19, 2001.

relationships among involved family members, including the baby's father. Because the nurses visit frequently during the prenatal period and continue their visits for two years following the birth of the child, they often form close bonds with the mother, her child, and other family members. Sometimes these close bonds enable them to better help families with complex and deeply engrained problems by modeling appropriate behaviors. ...

"Perhaps, most typically, is the case of Kaylene,[2] an 18-year-old who was 14 weeks pregnant and had just graduated from high school. 'This was not a planned pregnancy,' states her PHN, 'and her family disapproved of her pregnancy and her boyfriend.' Kaylene found a part-time job, continued to attend all her prenatal appointments, and accepted her Nurse's referral to WIC [the Woman, Infants, Children program] for food assistance, as her low-paying job did not adequately cover all her expenses. Family conflict occurred when Kaylene's ex-boyfriend, who had initially broken up with her because of the pregnancy, re-entered the picture, which outraged the family. After Kaylene delivered a term male infant with her mother and boyfriend at her side, she was asked to leave home because she was continuing her relationship with the baby's father. The PHN worked with Kaylene and her family, [which] enabled her to stay with her parents until she could become self-sufficient. With the encouragement of the PHN, she enrolled in a local ROP [Regional Occupational Program] and applied to begin classes in medical assistance training that also provides job placement following graduation. Kaylene is grateful that her nurse 'supported her in her decisionmaking in such a non-judgmental way,' and she never misses an opportunity to thank her nurse for her help."

PROJECT 25: OPERATION READ[3]

"Anna[4] is a recent sixteen year old Operation READ graduate from the New Directions for Youth (NDY) office in Van Nuys. When she came to NDY in early April of 2001 Anna was living from place to place, spending each night at a different friend's house and was essentially homeless. With a reading level of below fourth grade, she had very little chance of 'making it' in the world, and so,

[2]The client's name was changed to protect her privacy.
[3]Memo from Elias G. Rivera, Operation READ Tutoring Counselor, New Directions for Youth. November 15, 2001.
[4]The client's name was changed to protect her privacy.

with the encouragement of her friend, she decided to bring her life around and attend the Operation READ Program.

"The Tutoring Counselor at the time was able to get through to Anna and gave her motivation to attend the Operation READ sessions regularly. With hard work and dedication, Anna was able to raise her reading level to almost that of a seventh grader by August of that same year. By October, she had completed her 80 hours required by the program and enrolled in NDY's GED classes.

"Even though Anna has finished the Operation READ Program, she continues to come into the office and help the current Tutoring Coordinator with office chores, turning herself into a volunteer and giving back to the program that gave to her. The new duties as a volunteer have given Anna a renewed self-perception that can be seen in the way she acts, speaks, dresses, and interacts with others. Anna is a true inspiration and a testament to the enduring human spirit that sometimes just needs a hand to get itself back in the right direction."

DISCUSSION

The goal of investing public money in an effort such as the LTFSS Plan is to help families achieve self-sufficiency and to do so by targeting five outcome areas for intervention: good health, economic well-being, social and emotional well-being, safety and survival, and education and workforce readiness. The idea is that by investing these funds today, less will be spent in the future on remediation. However, the cost of failure is not just the public funds expended on programs to "clean up the mess," such as the costs of welfare, emergency room care, or imprisonment. It is also the waste of the unexploited potential of a generation or more of children. The LTFSS Plan and other similar efforts in the County to assist low-income families and children intend to reduce societal costs and improve the outlook for future generations.

3. RESULT AND OUTCOMES

INTRODUCTION

In this chapter, we list the desired result of the LTFSS Plan and the five outcome areas the LTFSS Plan was intended to address. We then discuss the 26 indicators within the five outcome areas and the selection of the five headline indicators that are the focus of the discussion in Chapter 4. The material for this chapter is drawn from Hedderson and Schoeni, 2001; readers are referred to that document for a more in-depth discussion.

RESULT

The LTFSS Plan envisions 46 interrelated projects working toward a single result: *sustained self-sufficiency for CalWORKs families, former CalWORKs families, and other low-income families in Los Angeles County.*

OUTCOME AREAS AND INDICATORS

The Board's instructions to the NDTF were to create "strategies that provide maximum effectiveness to stabilize families by building their capacity to become self-sustaining." To do so, and following the RBDM Framework, the NDTF began by identifying measurable indicators. These indicators were to:

- Guide future planning and program decisions by focusing on positive outcomes for families;
- Broadly reflect the various aspects of Long-Term Family Self-Sufficiency; and
- Be measurable through qualitative and/or quantitative data, which is currently available or can be readily generated.

The NDTF identified 26 indicators, displayed in Table 3.1. They are grouped according to the Board's five outcome areas: Good Health; Safety and Survival; Economic Well-Being; Social and Emotional Well-Being; and Educational and Workforce Readiness. Indicator data will be used to assess the success of the LTFSS Plan as a whole by tracking progress toward the Plan's result and outcomes.

Table 3.1
Initial List of Outcome Areas and Indicators for the LTFSS Plan

Outcome Area	Indicators
Good Health	**Low birth weight births (-)** Access to health care (+) Infant mortality (-) Births to teens (-) Individuals without health insurance (-)
Safety and Survival	**Domestic violence arrests (-)** Child placement in out-of-home care (-) Juvenile probation violations (-) Successful minor/family reunification after out-of-home placement (+) Youth arrests for violent crimes (-)
Economic Well-Being	**Annual income under Federal Poverty Level (-)** Adults employed by quarter (+) Percent of family income used for housing (-) Access to transportation (+) Adults earning a living-wage (+) Homeless "episode" within prior 24 months (-)
Social and Emotional Well-Being	**Personal behaviors harmful to self or others (domestic violence, child abuse/neglect, substance abuse) (-)** Access to quality child care (+) Participation in community activities (voting, volunteering, mentoring, church, etc.) (+) Parent-child time together (+)
Education and Workforce Readiness	**Teenage high school graduation (+)** Adult educational attainment of high school diploma, GED, or eighth-grade reading level (+) Elementary and secondary school students reading at grade level (+) Mother's educational attainment at child's birth (+) High school graduation among mothers who gave birth before graduating high school (+) Adult participation in education or vocational training (+)

NOTE: Parenthetical sign indicates desired direction of impact.

HEADLINE INDICATORS

Because there are a large number of indicators, the County decided it needed to focus on one indicator from each outcome area to serve as a headline indicator (listed in bold in Table 3.1). In this section, we summarize the analysis (captured fully in Hedderson and Schoeni, 2001) on why the five headline indicators were selected. Data sources are provided in Appendix B.

Criteria for Evaluating Indicators

The LTFSS Plan Evaluation Design defines three qualities of a good indicator: communication power, proxy power, and data power (Friedman, 2001). We discuss each below.

Communication Power. Indicators should clearly communicate to County employees and County residents how the County is doing. The measures should be powerful, common sense, and compelling, not arcane and bureaucratic. An example of an indicator with strong communication power for the outcome area of education/workforce readiness is teenage high school graduation. The general public can understand this indicator, and most people have experienced it.

Proxy Power. Proxy power concerns the degree to which the indicator measures something of central importance about self-sufficiency or one of the five outcome areas. An example of proxy power is again teenage high school graduation rates as an indicator of the education and workforce readiness outcome. This indicator is expected to correlate with the other indicators within this outcome area, such as adult attainment of high school diploma, elementary and secondary school students reading at grade level, mother's educational attainment at child's birth, and high school graduation among mothers who gave birth before graduating from high school.

Data Power. Data power represents the validity and availability of the information necessary to calculate the indicator. An example of an indicator with high data power is the percentage of low birth weight births. This indicator is accepted as a valid indicator of the health of mothers and infants at the time of delivery. Data are available annually since 1960 for many levels of geography, from subcounty to national areas. This indicator can also be broken down by race/ethnicity and the education of the parents, and the necessary data to calculate the indicator can be acquired quickly.

Although the final LTFSS Plan indicators are good measures and the best available, they, like indicators for other program evaluations, have limitations. When rigorously scrutinized, any indicator will have some shortcomings. In terms of proxy power, any one indicator provides only a suggestion of what is happening in a broad outcome area, such as good health. In terms of validity, the statistics available for the indicators are subject to the errors that occur in collecting administrative information or conducting surveys. In terms of availability by time period, geographic breakdowns, CalWORKs and poverty status, and other socioeconomic characteristics, most of the indicators are uneven. The challenge is to devise analytical strategies that bridge the gaps in the data so that the evaluation does not become an incomprehensible, unconnected mixture of separate indicators, different time periods, and different groups of people.

4. BASELINE DATA AND THE STORY BEHIND THE BASELINES

INTRODUCTION

The LTFSS Plan has a broad Countywide perspective—long-term self-sufficiency for low-income families in the County. Moreover, in developing the Plan, the County attempted to use the RBDM Framework, since the RBDM Framework is a results-based accountability approach. An important component of the Plan is a Countywide Evaluation describing how successful the County is in achieving its goal. The RBDM Framework specifies a technique for doing so, which involves analyzing data over time on the 26 indicators that were determined to address the five outcomes of interest: good health; safety and survival; economic well-being; social and emotional well-being; and education and workforce readiness.[1] As discussed in Chapter 3, 5 headline indicators were selected from the 26 indicators.

First, historical trends in this baseline data are established. Second, the "story" behind those baseline trends is designed to explain what factors influence these trends. This story is developed using information from a variety of sources, including consultation with experts and review of the research literature that addresses which social, political, and economic factors are believed to influence the trend and how they do so. The next step is to determine the extent to which these factors have changed in the County. For example, the literature has shown that poverty is much higher for certain racial/ethnic groups; therefore, one can estimate the extent to which the racial/ethnic composition of the population in the County has changed in recent years. The changes in the factor—e.g., racial/ethnic composition—can be translated into the implied impact on the headline indicator—e.g., poverty—based on the relationships estimated in the research literature.

Trends in the data are then forecast into the future as if the LTFSS Plan had never been implemented. This is intended to show what might happen if the County did nothing. The historical trend, plotted through 2000 where available,

---

[1]If historical data are not available, the Framework instructs evaluators to construct an appropriate comparison group against which to measure outcomes.

is used to forecast what indicators would be in the absence of the LTFSS Plan. The methods and factors influencing the forecasts differ across indicators. As the Plan is implemented, these forecasts can be compared to actual outcomes in the year 2001 and beyond to measure County progress toward achieving its goals for low-income families.

This chapter presents estimates for the five headline indicators for the County corresponding to the five outcomes: low birth weight births (good health); domestic violence arrests (safety and survival); annual income under poverty level (economic well-being); personal behaviors harmful to self or others (social and emotional well-being); and teenage high school graduation (education and workforce readiness). For each headline indicator, we measure a baseline trend; describe the factors that are thought to have affected the baseline trend to appear as it does, i.e., tell the "story behind the baseline"; and provide forecasts into the future. Data for the secondary indicators are discussed briefly and are presented in more detail in Appendix B. The material for this chapter is drawn from Schoeni et al., 2001, although the data and forecasts have been updated; readers are referred to that document for a more in-depth discussion. In future years, this chapter will compare outcomes data to the forecasts to assess the progress the County has made toward achieving its goal.

GOOD HEALTH

Low Birth Weight Births

As shown in Figure 4.1, the percentage of infants born weighing less than 2,500 grams—the low birth weight rate—increased in the County during the 1990s. The increase in the percentage of low weight births is not unique to Los Angeles; it has been observed for the rest of California and the nation as well. Figure 4.2 shows that the County had a higher rate of low birth weight births than does the rest of the state, but both are well below the national average.

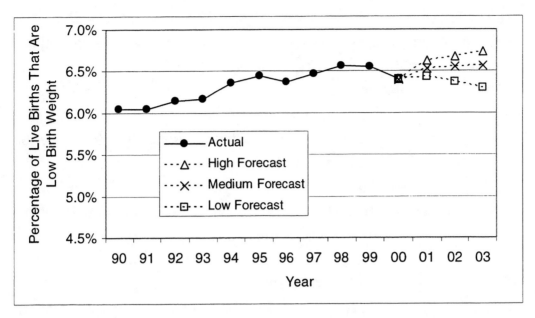

Figure 4.1—Low Birth Weight Births in Los Angeles County: 1990–2000 and Forecasts

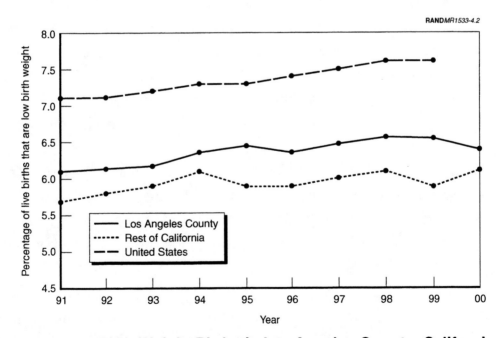

Figure 4.2—Low Birth Weight Births in Los Angeles County, California, and the Nation

The increase of the 1990s represents a departure from improvements in low birth weight rates that were made nationally during the 1960s and 1970s. Increases in the percentage of infants born with low birth weight are of concern because such infants face an elevated risk of a wide variety of health and developmental problems or conditions. In addition, low birth weight significantly increases the risk of infant mortality (Hack et al., 1995; Paneth, 1995).

The results further indicate the following:

- The increase in low birth weight births during the 1990s can be attributed primarily to increases in the percentage of multiple births. Twins, triplets, and higher-order births tend to be born at much lower weights than single births. The percentage of multiple births increased 25 percent during this time period.
- The low birth weight birth rate among single births has remained relatively constant over the same time period.
- Although estimates of the low birth weight birth rate are not available for CalWORKs participants, it is expected that this rate did not increase during the 1990s for lower-income women, such as those on CalWORKs. This conclusion is based on the fact that the increase in multiple births was largely the result of an increase in the use of fertility treatments, which are mostly used by higher-income women. Future analysis will attempt to directly examine low birth weight births among CalWORKs participants.
- The prevalence of maternal behaviors that are associated with low birth weight, such as smoking or drinking during pregnancy, has declined nationally. There are no data available to determine whether this healthy trend differs in the County.
- Shifts in the racial/ethnic composition of the population in the County do not explain the increases in the rate of low birth weight births in the 1990s.

To try to understand the likely future path of low birth weight, we provide three forecasts, as shown in Figure 4.1. The three forecasts are based on different assumptions. Our first forecast, labeled "medium," provides a linear extrapolation from the more recent births, 1994–2000. Our second forecast, labeled "high," provides a linear extrapolation based on all of the data for 1991–2000. Finally, our third forecast, labeled "low," provides a quadratic or curvilinear extrapolation based on all of the data for 1991–2000.

The range of the estimates is less than half a percentage point. The medium estimate is between these two at 6.4. The low estimate projects the low birth weight birth rate as holding fairly steady at 6.3 percent. The high estimate implies a slight increase in the low birth weight birth rate, from 6.3 percent in 2000 to 6.7 percent in 2003.

Other Indicators of Good Health

Unlike the low birth weight indicator, the other indicators used to measure progress toward the goal of good health generally show improvements over the last decade. Table 4.1 reports Countywide estimates for each nonheadline indicator, with more detailed estimates and data sources listed in Appendix B. The infant mortality rate in the County fell from 7.72 infant deaths per 1,000 live births in 1991 to 5.95 in 1997. Similarly, the birth rate for teenage girls age 10 to 17 fell significantly during the 1990s, from 20.7 in 1991 to 12.5 in 1999. These improvements have been seen across all racial/ethnic groups.

Table 4.1 Nonheadline Indicators for Good Health in Los Angeles County: 1990–1999

Indicator	90	91	92	93	94	95	96	97	98	99	00
Deaths to babies under 12 months per 1,000 live births		7.7	7.4	7.2	7.0	6.7	5.9	5.9			
Births to women ages 10-17 per 1,000 women ages 10-17		20.7	20.0	19.6	19.3	18.7	16.9	15.2	13.8	12.5	
Percent of persons without health insurance	16.2	26.2	26.9	26.1	29.1	28.9	27.5	29.1	30.1	28.8	

The percentage of individuals in the County who do not have health insurance is the exception, showing a general upward trend since the mid-1980s.

This increase in the percentage of people without health insurance can be partly explained by the demographic changes that have occurred in the County. Based on data from the California Department of Finance (CDF), the Hispanic population, which is most likely to be uninsured, grew from approximately 36 percent of the population to 45 percent from 1989 to 1999.

SAFETY AND SURVIVAL

Domestic Violence Arrests

The arrest rate for domestic violence has been increasing in the County over the last decade, as shown in Figure 4.3. Between 1988 and 1997, the total number of arrests per year increased 38 percent. However, because population grew as well, the domestic violence arrest rate—measured as the number of arrests per 100,000 population age 18 and over, and as shown in the figure— grew at a slightly slower rate, from 197.6 to 276.7 between 1988 and 1997. The arrest rate then declined, such that by 2000, the arrest rate per 100,000 was 211.7.

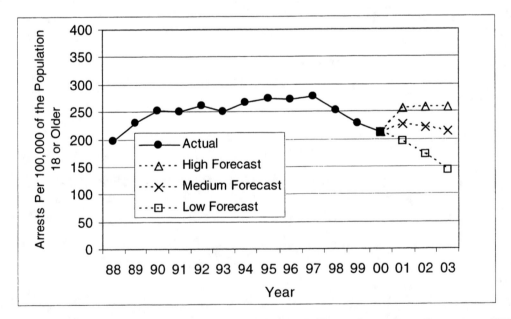

Figure 4.3—Domestic Violence Arrest Rate in Los Angeles County: 1988– 2000 and Forecasts

This trend toward more arrests until 1997 and falling thereafter has been observed for the rest of the state as well. In the early 1990s, the arrest rate in the County was 30 to 40 percent higher than it was for the rest of the state, as shown in Figure 4.4. In recent years, this gap has narrowed, to the extent that in 2000, the arrest rate in the County was only 4 percent higher than it was for the rest of the state, largely because of the rapid growth in arrest rates elsewhere in the state.

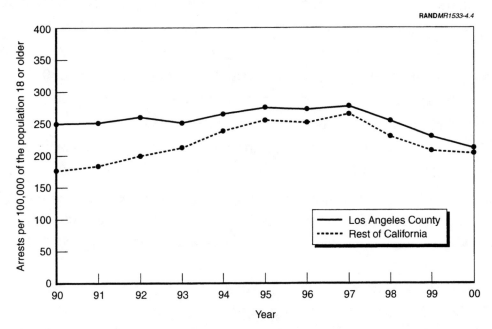

Figure 4.4—Domestic Violence Arrest Rate in Los Angeles County and California

Arrest rates for domestic violence reflect three distinct components: (1) the number of domestic violence incidents; (2) the willingness of victims and witnesses to report an incident; and (3) police behavior once police receive a report of an incident.

The observed increases in the domestic violence arrest rate in the early 1990s can be viewed as an improvement because it appears to be driven by positive changes in police behavior. During this time period, California initiated a number of changes specifically targeted toward increasing police use of arrest in domestic violence situations. In addition to legislative efforts, many local organizations have been established to address domestic violence. Other efforts have focused on improving police response. The subsequent decrease is difficult to explain. According to data from the National Crime Victimization Survey (NCVS), domestic violence toward females has been on the decline since 1993 (Greenfeld et al., 1998; Rennison, 2000). While we do not have data specific to California, this national trend suggests that domestic violence incidents may have also been in decline in the County. This may be driving the decrease in the arrest rate, though more evidence is needed.

Three forecasts are provided in Figure 4.3, based on three different assumptions. The first forecast—"medium"—assumes a curvilinear (quadratic) trend over the entire 1988 to 2000 time period. The second forecast—"low"— assumes that the recent and future trend is accurately represented with a quadratic specification over the more recent data from 1995 to 2000. The third forecast—"high"—assumes that a linear trend over 1988 to 2000 is the most appropriate characterization of the indicator.

The medium estimate implies that the arrest rate will continue to fall consistent with the trend that occurred between 1997 and 2000. With this forecast, the arrest rate would reach 143 by 2003. The low estimate projects a fall in the arrest rate from 211 in 2000 to 57 by 2003. The high estimate has arrest rates following their decade-long path and rising to 258 by 2003.

Other Indicators of Safety and Survival

Table 4.2 reports Countywide estimates for each nonheadline indicator, with more detailed estimates and data sources listed in Appendix B. The observed trends in the other indicators of safety and survival are consistent with the story that the increase in domestic violence arrests reflects changes in police behavior rather than an increase in the actual number of domestic violence incidents in the community. That is, all other indicators have shown improvements in recent years. The homicide rate (number of homicides per 100,000 population), the youth arrest rate for violent crimes (number of arrests per 100,000 youth), and the child placement in out-of-home care (number of placements per 1,000 children) have fallen considerably during the 1990s.

As discussed above, homicide rates are considered a good indicator of violent crime trends in communities. In part, this reflects the fact that homicides are more likely to be reported to police than domestic violence incidents. As a result, it is generally thought that changes in homicides are more reflective of changes in the number of actual incidents occurring than in police behavior once an incident is reported. Taken together, the indicators of safety and survival show improvements over the last decade. These trends suggest that changes in police behavior more than changes in the actual number of domestic violence incidents explain the upward trend in arrests for domestic violence, and that the most recent decrease in the arrest rate may be driven by a decrease in incidence rather than a decrease in police intervention.   However, more evidence is needed in this area.

Table 4.2 Nonheadline Indicators for Safety and Survival in Los Angeles County: 1990–1999

Indicator	90	91	92	93	94	95	96	97	98	99	00
Child placement in out-of-home care per 1,000 children (ages 0–18)	4.6	4.4	4.4	4.8	4.5	4.5	5.2	4.7	3.4	3.2	
Youth arrests for violent crime per 100,000 children under 18	1065	949	913	818	773	724	647	591	536		
Homicides per 100,000 persons	21.4	22.5	22.8	22.0	19.4	18.8	15.8	13.4	10.6	9.5	

ECONOMIC WELL-BEING

Annual Income under Poverty Level

As shown in Figure 4.5, the poverty rate—defined as the percentage of people living in families whose income is below the federal poverty threshold—has been declining rapidly since the mid-1990s. Almost 25 percent of Angelenos lived in poverty in 1994, but in the latest year for which data are available, 2000, 16 percent lived in poverty. Despite the substantial improvements since 1994, the long-run trend over the entire 25-year period for which data are available has been toward higher poverty.

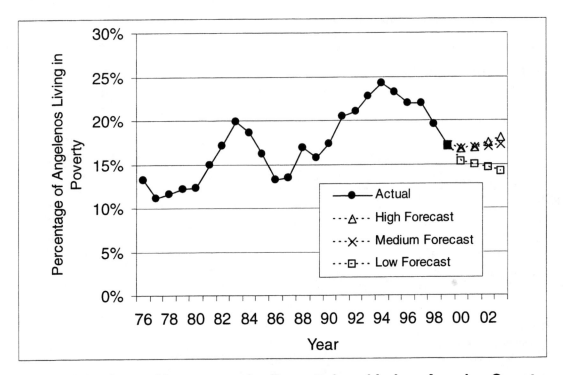

Figure 4.5—Annual Income under Poverty Level in Los Angeles County: 1976–2000 and Forecasts

As shown in Figure 4.6, poverty rates in the rest of California and in the nation are fairly similar, while the poverty rate in the County is considerably higher. This is partly because of different populations that make up these geographic regions, which also can explain the trends over time. The long-run increase in poverty can be viewed in terms of the racial/ethnic composition of the population. Compared to 25 years ago, a higher percentage of Angelenos today are Hispanic, a racial/ethnic group with a high poverty rate.

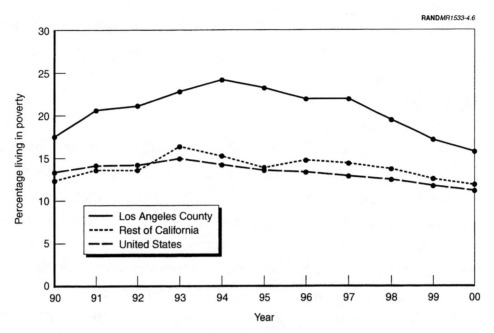

RAND*MR1533-4.6*

Figure 4.6—Annual Income under Poverty Level in Los Angeles County, California, and the Nation

Short-run fluctuations in poverty result primarily from changes in the macroeconomy. In addition, some of the recent decline is likely associated with changes in welfare policy. Although the latest data is for 2000, we expect that poverty continued to fall in 2001, given that the economy in the County expanded during the past two years. Poverty in the next few years will be heavily influenced by the economy, ongoing demographic changes, and welfare and poverty policy.

For each of the three forecasts displayed in Figure 4.5, the driving factor is the strength of the economy as represented by the unemployment rate. First recall that the latest measurement of poverty is for 2000. However, the unemployment rate for the County has been measured more recently. Therefore, we can use the historical relationship between the unemployment rate and the poverty rate, along with the actual unemployment rate in 2000 and 2001, to predict poverty in 2001. We then extend the predictions of the poverty rate into the future based on alternative predictions of the economy (i.e., unemployment rate).

The "medium" estimate is based on the assumption that the unemployment rate in 2002 will be 5.8 percent and 6.0 percent in 2003, which is 0.2 and 0.4 percentage points higher than the (seasonally adjusted) rate for July 2001. The unemployment rate is translated into a change in the poverty rate based on estimates in the research literature, which suggest that a 1 percentage point increase in the unemployment rate translates into (at most) 0.7 percentage points higher poverty.

The "low" prediction assumes that the economy will expand slightly (i.e., the unemployment rate will fall to 4.7 percent by 2003, which was roughly the national rate in July 2001). Moreover, it is assumed that there will be additional gains in poverty consistent with the large unexplained declines in poverty that have occurred in the past four to five years. That is, the fall in poverty between 1994 and 2000 is greater than can be explained by the fall in unemployment. Therefore, we assume that this unexplained portion will continue to place downward pressure on poverty. The final "high" estimate is based on the exact same approach as the one used for the "medium" estimate, except that a somewhat more pessimistic forecast is made for the economy. Instead of the unemployment rate increasing to 7.2 percent by 2003, it is assumed that the rate increases to 7.2 percent, or the level that existed in the last recession in (roughly) 1996.

All three estimates imply that poverty falls between 2000 and 2001. The low estimate implies a continual fall in poverty through 2003, reaching a rate of 14 percent in 2003. The less optimistic scenarios imply poverty rising beginning in 2001 and reaching 18 percent in 2003.

Other Indicators of Economic Well-Being

In addition to poverty, data are available for adults employed and percentage of income used for housing. Table 4.3 reports estimates for these nonheadline indicators, with more detailed estimates reported in Appendix B. Adults employed is defined as the percentage of adults 18–61 who were employed at any point during the calendar year.[2] Housing costs as a percentage of income are measured as the ratio of the average spending on all housing costs to average household income. Housing costs include the cost of

[2]Hedderson and Schoeni (2001) proposed estimating employment by quarter, which was suggested in the LTFSS Countywide Evaluation Plan. However, quarterly estimates are not available by income and CalWORKs status; therefore, we provide annual estimates that are based on data that allow reporting by income and CalWORKs status.

electricity, gas, fuel, oil, garbage and trash, water and sewage, real estate taxes, property insurance, condo fees, land or site rent, and mortgage payments. The remaining three of the six indicators of economic well-being are on the Data Development Agenda.

Employment rate and housing costs as a percentage of income follow trends similar to poverty. That is, as the economy grew in the mid- to late 1990s, the employment rate in the County also increased. Between 1993 (the peak of the recession) and 1999 (the most recent annual data), employment rose from 72.5 percent to 77.5 percent. As noted earlier, CalWORKs participants experienced large increases in employment. Similarly, employment among people living in poverty increased from 41.9 percent in 1993 to 45.6 percent in 1999.

Table 4.3 Nonheadline Indicators for Economic Well-Being in Los Angeles County: 1990–1999

Indicator	90	91	92	93	94	95	96	97	98	99	00
Percentage of adults 18–61 employed any time during the year	78.2	76.2	74.9	72.5	73.9	74.0	74.5	76.3	76.9	77.5	79.2
Percentage of income used for housing		21.9		24.3		24.1		22.9		20.8	

Housing costs as a share of income typically decline when the economy expands, and this was the case in the late 1990s. Data are available every other year from 1991 through 1999, and over that period the fraction of income spent on housing rose and then fell back to approximately its 1991 level. However, CalWORKs participants spend a much higher fraction of their income on housing: Among people on CalWORKS, the share of income spent on housing costs was 29 percent in 1991 and 30 percent in 1999. This high level of spending as a percent of income is consistent with the notion that there are a minimum set of expenditures on items that are required to survive—housing, food, clothing—and even though expenditures on these items is lower for lower-income families, even the lowest-quality housing is expensive relative to income for these families. The most likely explanation for the rise and decline between

1991 and 1999 overall and among CalWORKS participants is the recession followed by an increase in employment and earnings, especially among welfare participants. In addition, changes in the treatment of earned income of welfare recipients and in the level of the benefit, and CalWORKs welfare-to-work programs, have all probably played a role.

SOCIAL AND EMOTIONAL WELL-BEING

Personal Behavior Harmful to Self or Others

Personal behavior harmful to self or others is measured with child abuse and neglect, which, in turn, is defined as the number of substantiated child abuse and neglect cases per 1,000 children in the population. Figure 4.7 shows that child abuse and neglect declined in the County during the 1990s, but the decline was not monotonic. Between 1990 and 1992, the rate fell from 32 to 23 per 1,000. However, this fall was followed by a substantial rise to 37 by 1996. After 1996, the rate declined in each of the subsequent four years, leaving the rate at 15 per 1,000, or one-half the level that existed at the beginning of the decade.

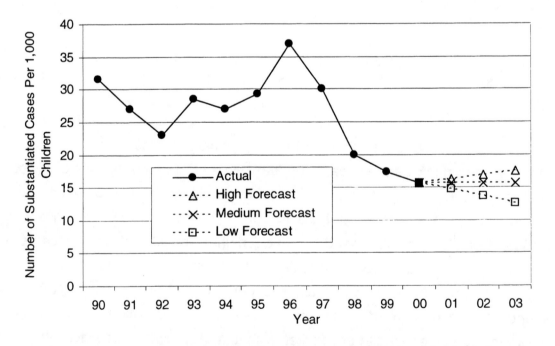

Figure 4.7—Child Abuse and Neglect per 1,000 Children in Los Angeles County: 1990–2000 and Forecasts

Changes in the rate of substantiated cases of child abuse and neglect can result from a change in reporting, a change in the response of child safety officials, and/or a true change in the incidence of child abuse. Each of these factors is affected by public awareness of preventive efforts and community and environmental trends.

It is not yet known for certain which aspects are reflected in the changes observed in the 1990s.

The recession of the early to mid-1990s, which caused an increase in poverty and a rise in welfare participation, was most likely an important cause of the increase in the child abuse and neglect rate in that it affected parental stress and, in turn, child safety. Similarly, the subsequent improvements in the labor market and poverty likely contributed to the decline in the late 1990s.

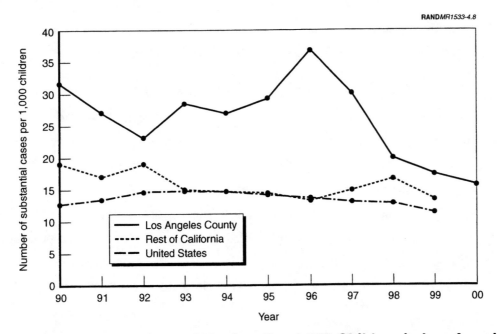

Figure 4.8—Child Abuse and Neglect Per 1,000 Children in Los Angeles County, California, and the Nation

At the beginning of the 1990s, the rate of substantiated child abuse and neglect was two-and-one-half times higher in Los Angeles County than in the rest of the nation, as shown in Figure 4.8. This gap declined substantially in subsequent years, with rates being 41 percent higher in the County than in the rest of the nation in 1999.

- 30 -

Three forecasts are reported in Figure 4.7 based on three different sets of assumptions. The "low" estimate assumes that the long-run (linear) decline in child abuse and neglect during the 1990s will continue to occur through 2003. The "medium" estimate is based on the assumption that the economy will hold steady at its current level (i.e., the unemployment rate will not change). The "high" estimate is based on the assumption that the key driving force behind changes in child abuse and neglect is the economy, and that the economy will weaken in the coming years. Specifically, it assumes that the unemployment rate of 5.4 percent in 2000 will increase to 7.2 percent by 2003, which is the level that existed in the County around 1998. Moreover, because the relationship between the unemployment rate and child abuse and neglect is not well established in the research literature, we estimate this relationship (using regression analysis) for the County using the data on these two outcomes during the 1990–2000 period. Based on this historical relationship and the assumed increase in the unemployment rate, a high estimate is projected.

Other Indicators of Social and Emotional Well-Being

In addition to child abuse and neglect, there are four other indicators in the social and emotional well-being outcome area. Three of them are on the Data Development Agenda. Thus, for the personal behavior harmful to self or others outcome area, participation in community activities is the only other indicator measured. The specific measure used for this report is the percentage of the voting-age population (18 and older) that voted in the most recent election. Countywide estimates for the 1996, 1998, and 2000 elections are reported in Table 4.4, with more detailed estimates and data sources provided in Appendix B.

Table 4.4 Nonheadline Indicators for Social and Emotional Well-Being in Los Angeles County: 1990–2000

Indicator	90	91	92	93	94	95	96	97	98	99	00
Percentage of voting age population that voted in November election							43.4		37.7		44.0
Percentage of voting age population that were registered to vote in November election							50.1		47.7		49.5
Percentage of registered voters that voted in the November election							86.8		78.9		89.0

Voting is historically substantially higher in presidential election years (1996 and 2000). Therefore, it is most useful to compare changes in voting in 1996 with 2000. There was virtually no change between 1996 and 2000, with roughly 44 percent of age-eligible voters turning out to vote in the County. These rates are much lower than they are for the rest of the nation, where in 2000, 65 percent of the voting-age population voted.[3]

The lower turnout rates in the County can be completely explained by the racial/ethnic composition of the population. Within each racial/ethnic group, Angelenos were at least as likely to vote as were people outside of the County. For example, although only 29 percent of Hispanics in the County voted in 2000, the same share of Hispanics outside of the County voted in that year. The large gap in age-eligible voting rates likely results from the fact that many Hispanics

[3]The population age 18 and over is considered age-eligible to vote. This measure does not consider other eligibility factors, such as citizenship. Further, it does not reflect voter registration. When these factors are considered, voter turnout in the County is quite similar to estimates for the nation.

and Asians are not citizens and, thus, are not eligible to vote. As evidence, among registered voters, the percentage that voted was slightly higher in the County than in the rest of the nation.

EDUCATION AND WORKFORCE READINESS

Teenage High School Graduation

We measure education and workforce readiness with the teenage high school graduation rate, which is defined as the ratio of the number of public high school graduates in a given year divided by the number of ninth graders in public schools three academic years earlier and expressed as a percentage. As Figure 4.9 shows, the high school graduation rate was virtually unchanged in the County during the period for which estimates are available, 1997–2000. The estimates imply that 62 percent of ninth graders graduate from high school within four years.

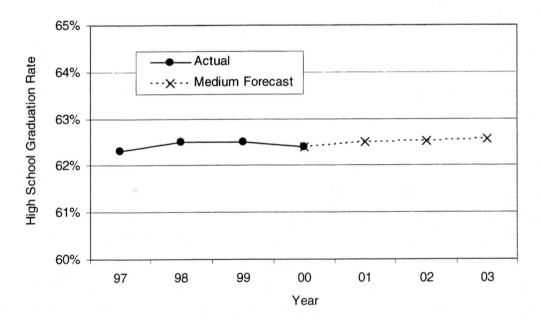

Figure 4.9—High School Graduation Rate in Los Angeles County: 1997–2000 and Forecasts

This rate is lower than the rate in the rest of California, where 71 percent of ninth graders in the 1996–97 academic year graduated in 2000. Although the graduation rate is higher in California, it follows a similar flat trend, as it does in the United States. Research suggests that the factors affecting high school completion include race/ethnicity, family income and background, labor market forces, and public policy. This is shown in Figure 4.10. These factors probably explain at least some of the difference between Los Angeles County, California, and the United States as a whole.

As noted above, data on the teen high school graduation rate are only available for 4 years, from 1997 to 2000. During this period, the rate was nearly constant (note the scale). We have no reason to believe that the rate will deviate significantly from the recent historical pattern. Therefore, we present only a "medium" forecast based on the linear trend between 1997 and 2000 (Figure 4.9). It implies a teen high school graduation rate of 62.6 percent by 2003, which is substantively the same as it was in 2000.

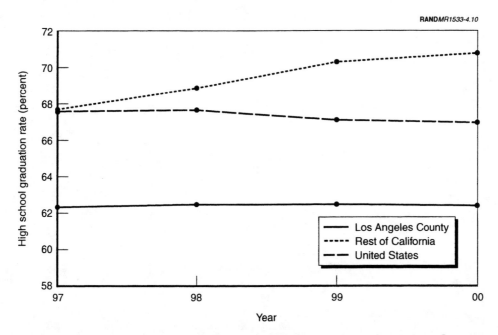

Figure 4.10—High School Graduation Rate in Los Angeles County, California, and the Nation

Other Indicators of Education and Workforce Readiness

Of the six indicators in the education and workforce readiness outcome area, just one was placed on the Data Development Agenda. As opposed to the headline indicator, three of the four remaining indicators show favorable trends. Table 4.5 reports the Countywide estimates of these nonheadline indicators, with more detailed estimates and data sources reported in Appendix B. Adult educational attainment, as measured by the percentage of adults ages 18 to 45 who have completed a high school degree or GED, increased gradually during the 1990s, from 70.2 percent in 1990 to 73.8 percent in 2000. Although we only have three years of data on how third graders are performing in the California Standardized Testing and Reporting program, we are seeing improvements. In addition, educational attainment of mothers giving birth increased by almost one full year, from 11.0 in 1991 to 11.7 in 1999. These improvements were experienced among all racial/ethnic groups, in all supervisoral districts (SDs), and in almost all eight service planning areas (SPAs).

Table 4.5 Nonheadline Indicators for Education and Workforce Readiness in Los Angeles County: 1990–2000

Indicator	90	91	92	93	94	95	96	97	98	99	00
Percentage of people ages 18–45 who have completed a high school degree or GED	70.2	72.2	73.4	72.9	72.9	72.1	72.9	72.0	72.1	73.7	73.8
Percent of 3rd graders performing at or above median for grade in the California Standardized Testing and Reporting program									29.0	31.0	34.0
Average years of education among women giving birth	11.0	11.0	11.1	11.1	11.2	11.3	11.5	11.6	11.7		
Percentage of people ages 18–45 who are enrolled in education or vocational training	17.0	15.3	15.9	16.3	14.4	18.3	18.2	17.7	17.7		

DISCUSSION

In summary, the baseline trends in the majority of the headline indicators (domestic violence arrests, poverty, and substantiated cases of child abuse and neglect) show general improvements during the 1990s. The percentage of low weight births and teenage high school graduation are the exceptions. The low birth weight rate increased during the 1990s and the teenage high school graduation rate was relatively constant across the years for which we have data.

This report provides the County with the baseline trends that will be used to compare performance as the LTFSS Plan is implemented and data on post-Plan outcomes can be measured. Project funding was available in Fiscal Year 2000–2001 (which began in July 2000).[4] Thus we use 2000 as the latest data with which to forecast future trends, comparing the trends to actual outcome data from 2001 and beyond. However, the LTFSS Plan is not likely to be fully implemented sooner than the end of 2002, which suggests that data are needed for at least 2002 and 2003 before complete post-Plan outcomes can be measured. In addition, delays in the release of data sources range from six months to two years, implying that estimates for 2002 and 2003 will be available no sooner than 2004 and, in many cases, not until 2005.

---

[4]County of Los Angeles New Directions Task Force, October 28,1999 letter to the Board of Supervisors: Recommendation to Approve Long-Term Family Self-Sufficiency Plan. This was approved by the Board of Supervisors on November 16, 1999.

5. THE PROJECTS AND THEIR PARTNERS

INTRODUCTION

This section of the report discusses the partners involved in the LTFSS Plan. The Countywide Evaluation that is the basis for this report is designed to address the first level of the two-level RBDM Framework: outcomes at the countywide level. The second level of the RBDM Framework concerns the 46 projects and the project evaluations that assess how well specific agencies and projects effect change for their clients. Because the LTFSS Plan is intended to create a synergistic effect in that together the projects will lead to better outcomes for low-income families, the Countywide Evaluation is charged with describing the projects. This includes summarizing information from the project evaluations including how they are thought to affect the indicators and whether projects can be expected to contribute to the Countywide outcomes. For similar reasons, the Countywide Evaluation is also charged with identifying public- and private-sector partners who are or should be playing a role in helping the County improve its outcomes for children and families.

In this chapter, we summarize the projects with respect to their indicators and discuss their potential impact on the indicators. However, as noted in Chapter 1, as of January 2002, only half the projects have begun delivering services to their clients, some of these only recently. It is therefore too early to incorporate the results from project evaluations, though many projects (and most of the implemented projects) have submitted their preliminary evaluation deliverables. Results from project evaluations will be included in next year's report. We also summarize the partnerships that have been developed as part of the LTFSS Plan. The material for this chapter is drawn from Schoeni et al. (2001) and Davis et al. (2001); readers are referred to those documents for a more in-depth discussion.

PARTNERS IN THE LTFSS PLAN

The LTFSS Plan is intended to address the needs of low-income families in Los Angeles County holistically. This is apparent in the Plan's Vision and Common Themes:

- "Where possible, services to families should support the family as a unit, rather than focusing on individual family members in isolation.
- Just as individuals live in families, families live in communities. Therefore, strengthening communities is an important part of strengthening families.
- Services are most effective when integrated at a community level.
- Focusing on positive outcomes for families is key to delivering effective services."

Thus, the Plan provides an overarching vision of bringing various agencies, service providers, and community members together. This makes the partnerships among these stakeholders a key part of achieving the Plan's goal of family self-sufficiency.

In addition, although the Plan originated with federal and state Temporary Assistance for Needy Families (TANF) and CalWORKs dollars, the money was not dedicated solely to the Department of Public Social Services (DPSS). Instead, the County formulated its desired result and outcomes, designed programs, and only then allocated across departments and agencies as required. This process was quite different from the more traditional stovepiping of departmental resources.

Our discussion of partners involved in the LTFSS Plan is derived from our analysis of the LTFSS Plan service-delivery and planning framework (Davis et al., 2001). The foundation of this analysis was a set of semistructured interviews with key informants. With the assistance of the Chief Administrative Office (CAO) and the DPSS, RAND identified knowledgeable potential interviewees, including County departmental staff from each of the lead agencies, DPSS staff responsible for planning and implementing the LTFSS Plan, CAO/Services Integration Branch (SIB) staff responsible for the evaluation of the LTFSS Plan, and non-County departmental participants, including advocacy groups, nonprofit organizations, and academics. RAND also collected and analyzed a wide range of written materials, such as planning documents, training materials, and official Board actions. These materials were augmented with broader perspectives from other ongoing RAND research on California welfare policy and the selection and implementation of social programs, as well as social science and management research drawn from the fields of organizational behavior, economics, and sociology.

WHAT WORKS? THE RELATIONSHIP BETWEEN PROJECTS AND INDICATORS

Considered individually, projects are not likely to have a measurable impact on the headline indicators. A project would have to be quite large and quite successful for it to change the historical trends in a county the size of Los Angeles County. While the success of the LTFSS Plan as a whole is based on "assessing conditions of well-being for children, families, and communities that are affected by multiple agencies and projects," project success is determined by "assessing how well specific agencies and projects perform" (Los Angeles County Long-Term Family Self-Sufficiency Plan Evaluation Design, October 23, 2000). However, in keeping with the global vision of the Plan, projects were designed to address collaboratively one or more of the outcomes and indicators specified in the Plan.

We begin our discussion of the projects with a list of the 46 projects that are funded by the LTFSS Plan, the outcomes they target, and the amount of funding that each has been allocated, as shown in Table 5.1.[1] Here, we discuss the projects associated with each outcome area.

Projects Targeting Good Health

Under the LTFSS Plan, 23 projects (12 under "Good Health" plus the 11 under "All Outcomes Areas") are expected to affect good health (see Table 5.1). Two of the projects are expected to affect good health's headline indicator—low birth weight: Project 10, Community Outreach to Increase Access to Health Care, and Project 34, Home Visitation Program. Project 10 helps pregnant women gain access to prenatal care and provides additional support services, such as parenting skill training, health education, and breast-feeding education. Through home visits by public health nurses, Project 34 will provide parenting education and support and provide referrals to other needed social services to young, first-time pregnant needy families and CalWORKs participants. These

---

[1]The material in this section is summarized from Schoeni et al. (2001).
[2]The material in this section is summarized from Schoeni et al. (2001).

projects expect to improve access to prenatal care and provide valuable information about proper nutrition and the behavioral risk factors associated with low birth weight births.

Table 5.1
List of Projects, Project Funding, and Outcome Areas Targeted by the Projects

Project Number and Name	Good Health	Safety and Survival	Economic Well-Being	Social and Emotional Well-Being	Education and Workforce Readiness	All Outcome Areas	Initial LTFSS Plan Funding ($m)
1. CalWORKs WtW Strategy			X		X		$4.00
2. Employer-Linked Education/Training			X		X		$2.50
3. Transitional Subsidized Employment			X				$0.00
4. County Apprenticeship Program			X		X		$0.00
5. Business Micro-Loan and Incubator			X				$1.00
6. Housing Relocation Program			X	X			$7.80
7. Strategic Info—Supp Job Creation			X				$0.33
8. Community Economic Development			X				$0.50
9. Mini-Career Centers			X		X		$1.50
10. Community Outreach—Health Care	X						$5.00
11. Hotline to Resolve Health Care	X						$0.00
12. Health Care Transportation	X						$0.00
13. Health First	X						$0.00
14. Transitional Support—Homeless			X				$9.48
15. Emergency Assistance—Eviction			X				$0.00
16. Housing Counseling/Training			X				$0.50
17. Community-Based Teen Services	X	X	X	X	X		$17.50
18. Teens with Special Needs	X	X	X	X	X		$2.50
19. Emancipated Foster Youth-Parents	X			X	X		$0.55
20. Teen Passport to Success	X	X		X	X		$0.74
21. Staff Dev for Teen Svc Providers	X			X	X		$0.50
22. Cal-Learn and Teen Parents					X		$2.40
23. Youth Jobs					X		$6.75
24. Public Library Services for Children					X		$0.68
25. Operation READ		X			X		$0.79
26. Safe Places	X	X		X	X		$2.40
27. DART/STOP for CW Families		X		X			$0.00
28. Domestic Violence Prevention		X		X			$0.65
29. School-Based Probation Supervision	X	X			X		$2.10
30. Support—Fam of Probation Child		X			X		$0.15
31. Strategic Support for Child Care				X			$5.00
32. Federal Family Supp Svcs Network						X	$4.50
33. LTFSS Family Preservation		X		X			$8.50
34. Home Visitation Program	X			X	X		$5.25
35. Peer Self-Help Support Groups						X	$0.28
36. Support and Therapeutic Options		X					$0.60
37. School Attendance Areas						X	$0.10
38. Multi-Disciplinary Family Inventory						X	$7.00
39. County Family Resource Centers						X	$1.35
40. Strategic Planning Data Centers						X	$0.58
41. SPA Council Staff and Tech Asst.						X	$0.64
42. CalWORKs Systems Review						X	$0.50
43. New Directions L-T Fam Comm						X	$0.00

44. CalWORKs Case Management						X	$0.00
45. TranStar Enhancement			X				$0.22
46. L-T Family Self-Suff Evaluation						X	$2.00
Total Number of Projects Related to Outcome	12	11	16	11	17	11	

In addition to the projects that seek to affect low birth weight, numerous projects under the LTFSS Plan are designed to improve access to health care in general: Project 11, Hotline to Resolve Health Care Access Issues, Project 12, Health Care Transportation, and Project 13, Health First. These projects can be expected to have an impact on low birth weight births through general improvements in health and greater access to regular preventive health care, but again, these effects are not expected to be very large.

Projects Targeting Safety and Survival

The criminal justice research literature can be used to make predictions about the potential impacts of the LTFSS Plan. Specifically, 22 of the projects under the LTFSS Plan are expected to affect safety and survival. Of them, two projects seek to impact the safety and survival's headline indicator—domestic violence in Los Angeles County: Project 27, DART/STOP for CalWORKs Families, and Project 28, Domestic Violence Prevention. Both projects focus on preventing domestic violence incidents.

The Los Angeles Police Department (LAPD) and the Los Angeles County Sheriff's Department have established emergency response teams in some areas to respond to domestic violence. Project 27 would link the existing CalWORKs Domestic Violence Program with the LAPD and Sheriff's Department response teams to facilitate access to services for CalWORKs participants who are victims of domestic violence.

Project 28 will develop a domestic violence risk assessment tool for use with CalWORKs participants. The assessment is intended to help determine individual risk of violence by an intimate partner. Participants will also be provided information about what to do if they are abused. In addition, the project will develop and distribute a domestic violence curriculum for teenagers in an effort to identify and prevent domestic violence among the young.

In addition to the projects that focus on domestic violence, other projects that improve economic well-being may have an impact on the incidence of domestic violence. Research shows that domestic violence is more common among lower-income women. Programs that improve income would be expected then to reduce the number of domestic violence incidents in Los Angeles County. Moreover, in 1998, the Board approved spending $12 million annually on domestic violence services to CalWORKs families, which may also influence observed trends.

Projects Targeting Economic Well-Being

Twenty-seven of the 46 LTFSS Plan projects intend to affect economic well-being. The strategy of many of these projects is to promote self-sustaining employment that will then generate enough income to move the family out of poverty and make them independent of government cash assistance. Here, we briefly describe the two largest projects (in terms of dollars allocated) that target the headline indicator for economic well-being—poverty.

Project 38, Multi-Disciplinary Family Inventory and Case Planning, will have each CalWORKs participant engage in a family inventory, where the family's strengths and needs will be assessed, including the family's involvement with County Departments other than the DPSS, including Probation, Department of Health Services (DHS), Department of Mental Health (DMH), Department of Children and Family Services (DCFS), and the Los Angeles County Office of Education (LACOE). Those families with higher level needs qualify. Seven million dollars is allocated to Project 38 during the five-year LTFSS Plan planning period.

Project 1 is an expansion of the CalWORKs Welfare-to-Work (WTW) Strategy, with $4.0 million in Single Allocation funding during the five-year LTFSS Plan planning period. The project builds on the Greater Avenues for Independence (GAIN) program while seeking to connect preemployment and postemployment services more effectively.

Projects Targeting Social and Emotional Well-Being

Twenty-two projects expect to affect social and emotional well-being. Of them, four with funding of at least $2 million during the five-year LTFSS Plan planning period expect to affect the headline indicator for social and emotional well-being—child abuse and neglect: Project 17, Community-Based Teen Services, is the largest LTFSS project and it plans to leverage together public schools, CBOs, County Departments, other public agencies, and parents and teens themselves to integrate services to help teens avoid pregnancy, graduate from high school, read at grade level, and reject violence.

The other three projects are Project 18, Teens with Special Needs, which also targets teens, specifically teens who are under represented; Project 26, Safe Places, which will establish places of safety within communities for children and youths to go during after school and non-traditional hours; and Project 38, Multi-Disciplinary Family Inventory and Case Planning, which was discussed above.

Projects Targeting Education and Workforce Readiness

Twenty-eight projects expect to affect educational and workforce readiness. Of them, 22 expect to affect the headline indicator—teen high school graduation. Among these 22 projects, Community-Based Teen Services, Project 17, has the largest funding at $17.5 million during the five-year LTFSS Plan planning period, and was discussed above.

Youth Jobs, Project 23, and Multi-Disciplinary Family Inventory, Project 38, are the two next largest projects. Youth Jobs will provide paid work-based learning opportunities for thousands of CalWORKs youths. The job experience is linked with functional basic skills enhancement, career planning, employment, employment readiness skills development, and job placement. The Multi-Disciplinary Family Inventory seeks to identify and address the human services needs, beyond traditional WTW activities, among CalWORKs participants.

The LTFSS Plan Encourages Both Public and Private Partnerships

The holistic approach of the Plan implies that many partners are involved with helping the County achieve its goals of self-sufficiency for children and families, though the process is predominantly led by County agencies. This can be seen in the number of collaborators for the various projects, as shown in Table 5.2, which summarizes the relationships between lead agencies and other entities across the individual projects. Lead agencies can provide services, and may also play supporting roles to other projects, including:

- Serving as service providers for other projects;

- Co-locating staff with other departments or agencies as part of an LTFSS project or having staff that comprise part of multi-disciplinary teams;
- Having treatment providers who may be affected by other LTFSS projects (e.g., referrals will be made to these providers);
- Co-leading an LTFSS project with another lead agency;
- Providing technical support to other projects (e.g., assistance with the development of monitoring tools).

Table 5.2
Partnerships among the LTFSS Plan Projects

Project No. and Name		Lead	Provider/Supporting Agency				
1	CalWORKs WtW Strategy	DPSS	Contr.				
1a	Career Plan and Prep Seminar	DPSS					
1b	Enhanced Appraisal	DPSS					
1c	Targeted Initial Job Search	DPSS					
1d	Part-Time Work w/ Educ/Training	DPSS					
1e	Voluntary Enhanced Motivation	DPSS					
2	Employer-Linked Educ/Training	DPSS	Contr.				
3	Transitional Subsidized Employment	DPSS	Contr.				
4	County Apprenticeship Program	DPSS	Contr.				
5	Business Micro-Loan and Incubator	CDC					
5a	Business Micro-Loan Program	CDC					
5b	Incubator Without Walls	CDC					
6	Housing Relocation Program	DPSS					
7	Strategic Info—Supp Job Creation	CDC	Contr.				
8	Community Economic Development	CDC	Contr.				
9	Mini-Career Centers	CSS					
10	Community Outreach—Health Care	DPSS	DHS	DMH	Contr.		
10a	1931 (b) Medi-Cal Outreach	DHS					
10b	Prenatal Outreach	DHS					
10c	CalWORKs Family Assistance	DPSS					
10d	Media Outreach	DPSS					
10e	Improving Inter-dept Capacity	DPSS					
11	Hotline to Resolve Health Care	DPSS	DHS	DMH	Contr.		
12	Health Care Transportation	DPSS	CAO/SIB	Other Depts			
13	Health First	DPSS					
14	Transitional Support—Homeless	CDC	Contr.				
14a	Relocation Grant—Homeless Families	CDC					
14b	Tenant-based Trans. Rental Asst.	Status Pending					
14c	Trans. Subsidized Employment	CDC					
15	Emergency Assistance—Eviction	CDC	Contr.				
16	Housing Counseling/Training	DPSS	Contr.				
17	Community-Based Teen Services	DPSS	Other Depts	Contr.			
18	Teens with Special Needs	DPSS	Other	Contr.			

Project No. and Name		Lead	Provider/Supporting Agency					
			Depts					
19	Emancipated Foster Youth-Parents	DCFS	Contr.					
20	Teen Passport to Success	DPSS	Contr.					
21	Staff Development for Teen Service Providers	DHS	Contr.					
22	Cal-Learn and Teen Parents	DPSS	Contr.					
22a	Teen Career Enhancement	DPSS						
22b	Career Counselors	DPSS						
23	Youth Jobs	CSS	Contr.					
24	Public Library Services for Children	Library	Contr.					
24a	Homework Center	Library						
24b	Teen Library Card Campaign	Library	Contr.					
24c	Support Services for After-School Program	Status Pending						
25	Operation READ	Prob.	DCFS	LACOE	Library	Contr.		
26	Safe Places	LACOE	Contr.					
27	DART/STOP for CW Families	CSS	Other Depts					
28	Domestic Violence Prevention	CSS						
28a	Risk Assessment Tool	CSS						
28b	Research: What Stops DV	CSS						
28c	DV Teen Curriculum	CSS						
29	School-Based Probation Supervision	Prob.	LAUSD	Indep School Distrs.				
30	Support—Families of Probation Child	Prob.		Contr.				
31	Strategic Support for Child Care	DPSS	Contr.					
31a	Child Care—Non-needy Caregiver	DPSS						
31b	Inc Non-traditional Child Care	DPSS						
32	Federal Family Supp Services Network	DPSS	DCFS					
33	LTFSS Family Preservation	DCFS	Prob	Contr.				
34	Home Visitation Program	DHS	Contr.					
34a	Nurse Home Visitation Program	DHS						
34b	Home Visitation and Case Management	DHS	Contr.					
35	Peer Self-Help Support Groups	DMH	Contr.					
36	Support and Therapeutic Options	Funded from another source						
37	School Attendance Areas	CAO/SIB	LACOE	Contr.				
38	Multi-Disciplinary Family Inventory	DPSS	DHS	DCFS	Prob	LACOE	DMH	Contr.
39	County Family Resource	DPSS	DHS	DCFS	Prob	DMH	Contr.	

Project No. and Name		Lead	Provider/Supporting Agency						
	Centers								
39a	County Family Resource Centers	DPSS							
39b	Deputy Prob. Officers for Family Resource Centers	DPSS	Prob						
40	Data Partnerships	CPC	CAO/ SIB						
41	SPA Council Staff and Tech Asst.	CPC							
42	CalWORKs Systems Review	DPSS							
43	New Directions L-T Family Self-Suff. Committee	DPSS	Other Depts						
44	CalWORKs Case Management	DPSS							
45	TranStar Enhancement	DPSS							
46	L-T Family Self-Suff Evaluation	CAO/ SIB	Contr.						

Note: Contr. – Contractor.

That there are many partners and that they work on projects contributing to more than one outcome area is made evident by examining who is involved with projects in each outcome area. For example, one of the Plan's five outcome areas is economic well-being. In the planning process, this workgroup was chaired by the Community Development Commission (CDC) and DPSS. The projects that contribute to this outcome area have several lead agencies, which provide services directly and partner with other agencies and service providers to deliver services.[3] The lead agencies include DPSS, CDC, and Community and Senior Services (CSS). In addition to the lead agency, a project may also work with both public and private organizations to deliver services to low-income families. As projects are implemented, they have or will involve partners beyond the lead agencies: Job Club contractors (such as the LACOE), Workforce Investment Boards, Department of Labor Welfare-to-Work Grantees, Community Colleges, Adult Schools, Regional Occupation Centers, the Department of Human Resources, SEIU 660, and CBOs.

---

[3]The direct service-delivery projects contributing to this outcome area are Projects 1–6, 8, 9, 14–18, 32, 34, and 35. Table 5.1 lists the projects by name and number. (*The Long-Term Family Self-Sufficiency Plan*, Los Angeles County New Directions Task Force, October 1999, pp. 92–93.)

Some of the same partners are seen in a second outcome area, good health.[4] In the planning process, this workgroup was chaired by DHS and DPSS, both of whom also serve as lead agencies on projects and as partners on projects for which they are not the lead. Service-delivery partners include (or will include, as projects are implemented): DHS, the Department of Mental Health (DMH), Medi-Cal 1931(b) outreach contractors, the Metropolitan Transit Authority, and CBOs.

Planning for the safety and survival outcome area workgroup was led by the DCFS and the Probation Department.[5] Services in this outcome area are also delivered (or will be delivered) by DPSS, school districts, community-based organizations, Job Club contractors, the Public Library, LACOE, Los Angeles Unified School District (LAUSD), local community colleges, LAPD and the Sheriff's Department, CSS, domestic violence service providers, and DMH.

The fourth outcome area is social and emotional well-being.[6] In the planning process, the Workgroup was led by DMH and DHS. Other direct service providers working or who will work in projects contributing to this outcome are DPSS, school districts, CBOs, DCFS, local community colleges, the National Family Life and Education Center, the Los Angeles County Public Counsel, Job Club contractors, LACOE, CSS, LAPD and the Sheriff's Department, CSS, domestic violence service providers, and child care resource and referral agencies.

The final outcome area is education and workforce readiness, which in the planning phase was led by LACOE and CSS.[7] Additional partners include DPSS, Job Club contractors, Workforce Investment Boards, Department of Labor Welfare-to-Work Grantees, Community Colleges, Adult Schools, Regional Occupational Centers, DHR, SEIU 660, school districts, CBOs, DCFS, local community colleges, the National Family Life and Education Center, the Los

---

[4]The direct service-delivery projects in this outcome area are Projects 10, 11, 13, 17–20, 26, 29, 32, 34, and 35.

[5]The direct service-delivery projects contributing to this outcome are Projects 17, 18, 20, 25–27, 30, 32, 33, 35 and 36.

[6]The direct service-delivery projects associated with this outcome are Projects 6, 17–20, 26, 27, 31–33, and 35.

[7]The direct service-delivery projects associated with this outcome are Projects 1, 2, 4, 9, 17–20, 22–26, 29, 30, 32, 34, and 35.

Angeles Public Counsel, CalLEARN contractors, the Public Library, the Probation Department, and DHS.

Some projects do not directly deliver services but contribute to all outcome areas. Most are part of the Plan's strategy for integrating the human services delivery system (Projects 37 through 46, though one project, TransStar Enhancement (45), also contributes to the economic well-being outcome area). The other projects (7, 12, 21, and 28) support one or more outcome areas. Partners working toward service integration include NDTF, CAO/SIB, and the Urban Research Division, DPSS, LAUSD, the CPC, DHS, DMH, DCFS, Probation, LACOE, and school districts.

The various partnerships are intended to have a synergistic effect on Countywide outcomes. They have also contributed to a certain degree of complexity, which, in part, has slowed implementation as relationships are established and formalized. We discuss this further in the next chapter, but the complexity of the relationships is summarized in Table 5.2. Thirty-five out of the 46 projects and subcomponents have at least one provider/supporting agency relationship, usually a contractor. Moreover, 12 of the 46 work with more than one provider/supporting agency, and Projects 38 and 39—Multi-Disciplinary Family Inventory and County Family Resource Centers—have six and five relationships, respectively. In addition, in the course of doing business, projects also coordinate with other entities not listed in this table, including the SPA Council, the Board, law enforcement agencies, school districts, city agencies or departments, colleges, Housing Authorities, private industry, planning bodies, and other organizations.

The County's progress toward a new approach to service delivery is by no means complete, as we will discuss in the next chapter, but many of the project participants we interviewed can already see changes in how the partnerships have affected the way the County delivers services. A number of benefits to the partnerships and the Plan were enumerated by interviewees, including:

- The shift in emphasis from individuals or specific service needs to a focus on the entire family encouraged County departments and agencies to work together to help needy families;

- Working together led to a growing level understanding of, and respect for, each other's programs and approaches to working with clients;
- Agencies were "forced" to become familiar with each other's programs, so that they are better able to make appropriate referrals for these families;
- Closer relationships between County departments/agencies and the community even resulted in closer collaboration on non-LTFSS Plan service delivery issues; and
- Improved understanding and communication developed between communities and agencies.

Several lead agencies commented that working with the LTFSS Plan target population is new to their departments. Their LTFSS projects have enabled them to begin developing new relationships with the community (as well as with other County agencies). These cooperative alliances are exactly what the Plan was designed to accomplish.

These results were neither easily achieved nor minor. In fact, it is important to acknowledge the scope and difficulty of that achievement. Coordination requires consensus-building and reconciling differences between lead agencies in departmental missions and mandates, professional cultures, and fundamental views about the approach for some projects. There are more practical concerns to consider as well. Co-locating staff or forming multi-disciplinary teams requires not only selecting sites and forming teams, but also addressing such issues as managerial structures and the sharing of client data. On a project where six lead agencies' personnel comprise the multi-disciplinary teams, we heard that, "[y]ou can multiply by three what is required to set up the administrative and supervisorial structures necessary to oversee these teams."

There are coordination challenges still to be resolved, and we discuss these issues in the next chapter. Nonetheless, many of the outstanding issues are those that face any entity seeking to integrate services, and the progress the County has made on this front should not be discounted.

6. ASSESSMENT OF THE LTFSS PLAN FRAMEWORK

INTRODUCTION

The LTFSS Plan has three stages: planning, implementation, and evaluation. Within these three stages, the RBDM Framework plays an integral role in planning and evaluation. (See Friedman, 2001.) In this chapter, we assess the utility of the RBDM Framework in terms of the planning component of the Plan and the effect of the resulting Plan on implementation. The RBDM Framework is a planning tool that emphasizes collaboration and partnerships, and does not provide guidance on implementation. Our discussion of implementation will therefore refer to the LTFSS Plan, and not to the RBDM Framework. In the next chapter, we assess the utility of the RBDM Framework for the evaluation component of the Plan.

The material in this chapter is drawn from Davis et al. (2001); readers are referred to that document for a more detailed discussion. That document also includes a more in depth discussion of the RBDM Framework. A complete presentation of the RBDM Framework can be found on the website of the Fiscal Policy Studies Institute. As was described in the last chapter, the research is based on RAND interviews with Plan participants as well as on an analysis of supporting materials (Board letters, training material, etc.) and the relevant research literature.

OVERVIEW OF GENERAL ISSUES

We begin our assessment of the utility of the RBDM Framework and the implementation of the LTFSS Plan with an overview of the general issues.

Background: The County and the Framework

In the County, as in most governments, planning and budgeting have traditionally had two features. First, planning occurs within limited domains. To deliver services, governments are organized into functional departments. This organizational structure, necessary for providing services, has the unintended and unfortunate effect of encouraging narrow planning within the individual organizations while discouraging coordinated planning across multiple departments and agencies. Therefore, the resulting programs tend to be narrowly focused based on the domain of the particular department or agency, ignoring interactions with other programs in other departments and agencies and creating a compartmentalized service delivery structure.

This compartmentalized service delivery structure is difficult for citizens to use. Instead of providing services in a "holistic way", the structure addresses each service issue and each family member separately. This tendency is reinforced both by standard bureaucratic considerations (e.g., the desire of senior bureaucrats to protect and expand their organizations) and by categorical external funding. Such categorical external funding usually flows to a particular department or agency (e.g., the designated welfare agency) and may be used only for specified purposes. Together, these factors discourage global planning across multiple departments and agencies and the integrated delivery of services.

The second feature of planning is that performance has traditionally been measured in terms of the effort expended rather than on ultimate outcomes. How many cases did the agency serve? What was the response time? Were there complaints? These narrow measures focus on the efforts of individual programs rather than "results"—i.e., effects on the client-level outcomes. This approach is imperfect because "trying hard is not good enough. We need to be able to show results to taxpayers and voters." (Friedman, 2001).

The RBDM Framework is intended to change these two traditional aspects of government planning and budgeting. It urges that planning start with ends and work backwards to means (Friedman, 2001). Specifically, this means that before selecting projects, planners should identify the population-level outcomes they want their programs to affect. These outcomes are then operationalized through the selection of specific indicators.

This focus on population outcomes then provides an overarching objective for planning and budgeting. Rather than focusing on individual funding sources and individual programs in isolation, the RBDM Framework's emphasis on population outcomes encourages global planning across programs and funding streams. How can we coordinate services provided by different departments to address these outcomes? How can we integrate services from multiple departments in a way that is seamless (or at least less fragmented than current practice)? How can we move funds coming into one department to the department that can best run the program that is most likely to affect the outcomes of highest priority? These ideas are expressed in the LTFSS Plan's common themes:

- Where possible, services to families should support the family as a unit, rather than focusing on individual family members in isolation.
- Just as individuals live in families, families live in communities. Therefore, strengthening communities is an important element of strengthening families.
- Services are most effective when integrated at a community level.
- Focusing on positive outcomes for families is key to delivering effective services.

These ideals are also expressed in the LTFSS Plan's commitment to think beyond narrow funding streams, as stated in the Plan:

Instead of figuring out how to comply with highly prescriptive federal or state regulations, we have had a rare chance to try to answer the most fundamental question we face: What programs and services will best help CalWORKs and other low-income families achieve Long-Term Self-Sufficiency?

Furthermore, relatively flexible CalWORKs Single Allocation funds and performance funds provided funding to implement this new holistic vision of service delivery.

In the RBDM Framework, the selected population outcomes and their corresponding indicators are used to select individual projects. Projects must then develop evaluations to assess their impact on client outcomes. Specifically, historical data on the outcomes are used to plot a "baseline," and this baseline is then used to project a trend in the absence of program intervention (i.e., a forecast of future levels of the indicator). Underlying this forecast is a "story behind the baseline" that incorporates an analysis of the forces that shift the indicator. This analysis is important for three reasons. First, it suggests causal paths through which programs might affect the indicator. Second, it suggests factors beyond simple extrapolation of recent trends that need to be considered in developing the forecast. Third, it helps to identify "partners," public and private-sector agencies that can help to affect the indicators.

Such partners are particularly important in the RBDM Framework approach. The RBDM Framework is explicitly and deliberately open. It emphasizes the importance of opening funding deliberations from narrow department and agency discussions to the broader community. It does so both because this makes for decisions that better reflect the preferences of the population, and because changing the indicators ("turning the curve") is viewed as a collaborative process between government, CBOs, and individual citizens.

Thus, in the planning stage, the community chooses a global action plan composed of individual projects. Ideally, the resulting projects are very different from "business as usual." They are developed with broad community input, rather than from within individual departments. As much as possible, funds flow from the departments nominally receiving the monies to the departments and nongovernmental organizations that can best implement the programs that are most likely to affect the population-level outcomes. Finally, the projects involve close coordination between the community and government departments.

Implementation

High-level planning for interdepartmental coordination is relatively easy. Senior management can make agreements among themselves. There is often attention (and implicit pressure) from global management (in the case of the County, the Board) for such coordination and cooperation. However, actual implementation of such cross-department efforts is likely to be more difficult because it takes place out of the spotlight of global management and involves a much larger group of people than just senior management. Therefore, a key issue in the final success of global planning efforts such as the LTFSS Plan will be how well such efforts succeed in keeping narrow department-specific considerations and priorities from redirecting or even derailing cross-departmental initiatives. Another challenge is to maintain community involvement and to try to ensure that the final project faithfully implements community intent.

The LTFSS Plan expresses four common themes:

- Where possible, services to families should support the family as a unit, rather than focusing on individual family members in isolation;
- Just as individuals live in families, families live in communities. Therefore, strengthening communities is an important element of strengthening families;
- Services are most effective when integrated at a community level;
- Focusing on positive outcomes for families is key to delivering effective services.

These themes often represented a change from standard County procedure. Thus, the Plan from the beginning implied major systemic changes. Several of the projects were new and therefore required activities and skills with which line staff whose primary responsibility is managing ongoing programs may have little experience or training.

The LTFSS Plan also moved funds from the receiving department to those that can best implement the programs. Yet, given the constraints imposed by the source of the funds, such flowing of funds, however, complicates implementation. Rather than one responsible department, there are now two (or more). The effort required to develop programs increases as a result. For example, implementation for several LTFSS programs cannot proceed until both departments and the Board approve the implementation plans, and such approval cannot occur until any disagreements about the plans have surfaced and are resolved. Doing so requires a high level of coordination by the two oversight groups. Delays because of coordination and priority setting should be expected.

Some projects (e.g., Project 38—Multi-Disciplinary Family Inventory) also encourage integration of service delivery at the caseworker/individual provider-level. To do so requires, in some instances, joint oversight of line operations and interconnection of lines of control, and that any decisions made by frontline staff be consistent with the regulations of both departments. Combined, these different levels of coordination can be time-consuming and require that interdepartmental procedures to address contractual, financial, and project administration be put into place.

THE USE AND UTILITY OF THE RBDM FRAMEWORK IN THE PLANNING PROCESS

In this section, we report the impressions of our key informants about the use and utility of the RBDM Framework in the planning process. We consider how the RBDM Framework was used in practice, what issues arose, how they were addressed, and what changes participants thought future applications of the RBDM Framework in the County should consider.

The RBDM Framework Succeeds in Focusing Attention on Ultimate Results

The RBDM Framework urges planners to begin by identifying the result(s) or outcome(s) they want to improve and to identify a list of outcome indicators that quantify the achievement of the outcomes; then, it urges planners to choose projects that they believe will improve those outcomes. Further, the RBDM Framework urges planners to involve all the relevant stakeholders in a collaborative process in deciding which result(s) and outcome(s) the Plan should achieve, and to select indicators to measure progress toward the outcomes.

The RBDM Framework is quite explicit about these goals, and, in practice, the LTFSS planners followed the RBDM Framework in defining the Plan's overall objective of helping families to achieve long-term self-sufficiency. Following Friedman's guidance, in the spring of 1999, a small task force convened by DPSS drafted a preliminary list of 45 outcome indicators that might be used to measure long-term family self-sufficiency. This draft set of indicators along with the RBDM Framework were presented at a May 1999 retreat that brought together a diverse group of County and non-County representatives from the County departments, major agencies outside of the County (e.g., LAUSD and LACOE), the City of Los Angeles, the CPC, SPA Councils, and selected community advocates and researchers. Retreat participants were asked to help develop a definition of "long-term family self-sufficiency" and to modify the draft set of measurable indicators based on the RBDM Framework.

Retreat participants reached a consensus on the definition of long-term family self-sufficiency and on reducing the draft list of 45 outcome indicators to a set of 26 indicators to measure progress toward the goal of achieving self-sufficiency for children and families. The 26 indicators were then grouped into five outcome areas—good health, safety and survival, economic well-being, social and emotional well-being, and education and workforce readiness.

Subsequent discussions about what programs would help the County achieve its goal of self-sufficiency for low-income families were then guided by this list of indicators.

In short, the RBDM Framework was used as intended and proved to be a useful planning tool: The planning process brought a wider array of perspectives to the table than has been the case in other planning efforts, and this new collaborative approach helped the County think broadly about what it wanted to achieve. Only after setting overarching goals would the County turn to the methods for achieving those goals.

Having a Longer Planning Process Would Have Made It Easier to Apply the RBDM Framework

The RBDM Framework does not specify a time frame over which planning should be accomplished, only that planning is an iterative process, in which results feed back into additional planning and efforts to refine the overall Plan and its component projects. Two other considerations urge a short planning period. First, funding streams have time-limited windows for use or commitment. Unspent funds are at risk of being reclaimed (or new follow-on funds not being allocated). Even when the Plan was being developed, such issues were clearly salient with respect to the PIF and SA funds which are the primary sources of LTFSS Plan funding. They have become more salient since then. Second, the earlier the money is spent, the earlier the citizens of Los Angeles County would benefit from their availability.

Consistent with these considerations, the County used its previous experience planning welfare reform as a guide, allowing six months for overall planning, including eight weeks for developing proposals.[1] The LTFSS planning leaders we interviewed commented that a lesson learned from the County's experience in planning for welfare reform was that a short, intensive planning process leads to quality products while keeping the engagement of the key players. Given this experience, these leaders had decided to undertake a similar

---

[1]The entire planning process for developing the LTFSS Plan spanned a little over six months, starting April 13 with the Board's instructions to the NDTF to begin the process and ending October 5 with the NDTF's adoption of the approved Plan.

planning process for the LTFSS Plan. They felt that six months was the longest period of time they could ask for to accomplish this task.

Following a May 1999 planning retreat, five Workgroups were created that corresponded to the five outcome areas.[2] The Workgroups were given eight weeks to develop project proposals and recommendations in the five outcome areas that are tied to the list of Countywide indicators. This focus on ultimate outcomes is in keeping with the RBDM Framework's intent; however, when interviewed, most Workgroup participants did not explicitly know about the RBDM Framework or recall using it. The Workgroup planning process for the most part appears to have followed the planning guidance outlined by the RBDM Framework.

Looking back on their experiences with the LTFSS Plan, many interviewees thought that in future applications of the RBDM Framework, the planning and project selection process would benefit from more time. They felt this would lead to a number of improvements including even wider community participation in planning and more thorough discussion of all possible options for spending the funds. We discuss the context for each of these areas for improvement in turn.

The RBDM Framework advocates broad community involvement in the planning process and calls for ensuring that all the key stakeholders are at the table. While there does appear to have been broad involvement of the community and non-County stakeholders in the May 21, 1999, meeting convened by the NDTF to develop a set of measurable indicators of "long-term family self-sufficiency," the Workgroup planning process that started in July, 1999, appears to have been less successful in maintaining a high level of community involvement. Further, there does not appear to have been strong overlap between the May retreat participants and those involved in the Workgroup planning process itself. Some of those participating in the early activities had left County employment or been assigned to other tasks. Thus, there was often little institutional memory of the community input that had been provided earlier. The resulting divergence between community input and final

---

[2]Subsequently, two additional Workgroups were created to address the needs of teens and integration of services.

Workgroup decisions appears, in some cases, to have frustrated community participants in the initial planning process.

The degree of community involvement also appears to have varied across the Workgroups. For example, about a third of Workgroup planning participants (including representatives of community groups, academics, and County employees) interviewed felt that the meetings and the selection of proposed projects was dominated by individual County departments. Further, those participants usually felt that the process of assigning a lead agency for each project was also dominated by the County departments. In addition, they felt that DPSS had a strong influence on the final selection of projects. Then again, six participants felt that community advocacy groups in several Workgroups had particularly strong voices in the planning process and were successful in getting their proposed projects adopted.

The second suggested area that could benefit from an extended planning period concerned funding decisions. Another consequence of the short planning phase was that there were alternative views about how the funds might be used —views that that some Workgroup participants did not feel were fully addressed and that might have been had there been more time. For example, interviewees expressed a variety of opinions about how to spend PIF dollars. Some advocated using the money to improve existing programs; others advocated funding fewer well-developed programs. The point is not that one view was right and another wrong, but that reconciling opposing views and building consensus, as the RBDM Framework guides, takes considerable time, more time than was allocated.

IMPLEMENTING THE LTFSS PLAN

In this section, we discuss the issues that arose in implementing the LTFSS Plan, what these imply for future global planning efforts, and the Plan's progress toward integrating the health and human services delivery system.

Adopting the LTFSS Plan Has Slowed Implementation

We begin with the result. The initial budgets for the projects had constant funding through the five budget years, implicitly assuming that projects would be provided services at their steady-state level early in the first year (i.e., soon after July 2000).

The reality has been quite different. The rollout of projects is proceeding slowly. For tracking purposes, the official DPSS *LTFSS Project Status Update* breaks the LTFSS Plan's 46 projects into 59 units (some projects are tracked at the subproject level; e.g., when lead responsibility for parts of the project are assigned to different departments). Table 6.1 provides the detail for 59 units from the April 2002 Status Update. Of them, 23 did not require Board approval, 18 were pending Board approval, and 18 had been approved (6 before July 2000, 10 between July 2000 and June 2001, and 2 since then). Similarly, 30 units are officially listed as not having begun providing services, with the remaining 29 providing services (3 starting before July 2000, 15 between July 2000 and June 2001, and 11 since July 2001). Even this figure for beginning to provide services sometimes provides an overly positive impression of the status of project rollout. Official Year-to-Date Expenditures as of February 28, 2002, imply that of the 38 non-DPSS projects (using an assignment of projects to departments slightly different than in the Project Status Update) only 7 spent any funds in the first year (July 2000 to June 2001) and only 2 more projects have spent any funds in the current year (i.e., through the reporting date, though there is reason to believe that that expenditure reports are incomplete). Furthermore, 6 of the projects listed as providing services are not listed as having any expenditures.

Table 6.1
LTFSS Project Status—April 2002

Project	Summary	Lead Agency	Funding	Dir. Svc. Yes/No	Board Memo Date	Board Letter Approv. Date	Implem. Plan Approv. Date	MOU Approval Date / Lead Agency Contract	Contracts (Start and End Date)	Sub-Contract	Service Start Date	Immigrant Planning Guide	Evaluation Plan (Due Date) / Completion Date
#1 CalWORKs Welfare-to-Work Strategy	Expands on the success of the current GAIN program linking pre-and post-employment services through an individualized approach through the combination of work, education and training. Emphasis is given to career planning, interest/skill appraisal, training, and job search.	DPSS	Single Allocation $4 million	Yes		3-02	N/A	N/A	New RFP released 5-17-01 Proposals received 6-20-01 Contracts approved	N/A	Target Date 8-02	Pending	Pending
#2 Employer-Linked Education/Training	Provides funding to make training and education available to participants and other low-income families in a setting linked to a particular employer.	DPSS	Performance Incentives $2.5 million	Yes	N/A	5-15-01	5-15-01	N/A	Contract Target 02-02	N/A	Pending	Pending	Completed 11-01
#3 Transitional Subsidized Employment/ Paid Work Experience	Subsidizes employment or paid work experience or enables participants to combine part-time employment with employer-linked education/training.	DPSS	Single Allocation $150,000	Yes	Target 6-02	N/A	N/A	N/A		N/A	12-5-00	Corrections returned 09-01	(3-5-01) Pending
#4 County Apprenticeship Program	Avails the participant to training through County employment potentially leading to full-time County employment.	DPSS	Single Allocation $900,000	Yes		N/A	N/A	Ground Maint. 8-7-00	LAUSD 8-7-00	N/A	Ground Maint. 12-5-00	Pending	Evaluation was approved 8-01

Project	Summary	Lead Agency	Funding	Dir. Svc. Yes / No	Board Memo Date	Board Letter Approv. Date	Implem. Plan Approv. Date	MOU Approval Date / Lead Agency Contract	Contracts (Start and End Date)	Sub-Contract	Service Start Date	Immigrant Planning Guide	Evaluation Plan (Due Date) / Completion Date
#5 Business Micro-Loan and Incubator Program for CalWORKs Participants	Provides a business micro-loan program for borrowers in possession of education and/or business training. Makes available free workshops, business development training, counseling and support for entrepreneurship.	CDC	Single Allocation $1 million										
5a. Business Micro-Loan Program for CalWORKs Participants	Provides a business micro-loan program for borrowers in possession of education and/or business training.	CDC	Single Allocation $500,000	Yes	Pending	N/A	N/A	Pending	N/A	N/A	Pending	Pending	Pending
5b. Business Incubator for CalWORKs Participants	Makes available free workshops, business development training, counseling, and support for entrepreneurship.	CDC	Single Allocation $500,000	Yes	Pending	N/A	N/A	Pending	N/A	Pending	Pending	Pending	Pending
#6 Housing Relocation Program	Provides one-time-only relocation assistance for participants in need of housing closer to employment, child care, or public transportation. A maximum of $1,500 may be used for moving expenses and utility and security deposits. Up to $405 is allowed for the cost of a refrigerator/stove, if needed as a result of the move.	DPSS	Single Allocation $7.8 million	Yes	9-25-00	N/A	N/A	N/A	N/A	N/A	9-18-00	Pending	(3-5-01) Submitted to SIB 6-5-01 Approved 4/8/02

Project	Summary	Lead Agency	Funding	Dir. Svc. Yes / No	Board Memo Date	Board Letter Approv. Date	Implem. Plan Approv. Date	MOU Approval Date / Lead Agency Contract	Contracts (Start and End Date)	Sub-Contract	Service Start Date	Immigrant Planning Guide	Evaluation Plan (Due Date) / Completion Date
#7 Strategic Information and Technical Assistance to Support Targeted Job Creation Activities	Involves research to determine steps to link current and potential occupations of CalWORKs participants with available businesses and industries. Focus will be upon those industries that can provide the most employment opportunities to CalWORKs participants.	CDC	Single Allocation $325,000	No	Pending	N/A; *(a letter will be required for consul-tant.) Pending	N/A	Pending	N/A	Pending	Pending	Pending	Pending
#8 Community Economic Development Initiatives	Provides community-based organizations with the opportunity to create jobs in their communities that are geared toward the skills and interests of CalWORKs participants while simultaneously strengthening the local economy.	CDC	Single Allocation $150,000 and Performance Incentives $350,000	Yes	N/A	Pending	Pending	Pending	N/A	Pending	Pending	Pending	Pending
#9 Mini-Career Centers	Locates centers in each of the eight SPAs to provide employment and postemployment services. These centers collaborate with the One Stop Career Centers and provide career services, counseling, and mentoring.	CSS	Single Allocation $1.5 million and Performance Incentives $500,000	Yes	N/A	1st Year 7-11-00; 2nd Year 6-19-01	1st Year 7-11-00; 2ndYear 6-19-01	Signed 8-01	N/A	7-01 to 6-30-02	2 SPAs up in 8-01; 3 SPAs up in 9-01; 2 SPAs up in 10-01; Last SPA up in 11-01	Presented at Adv. Workgroup on 10-11-01	Completed 2/27/02

Project	Summary	Lead Agency	Funding	Dir. Svc. Yes / No	Board Memo Date	Board Letter Approv. Date	Implem. Plan Approv. Date	MOU Approval Date / Lead Agency Contract	Contracts (Start and End Date)	Sub-Contract	Service Start Date	Immigrant Planning Guide	Evaluation Plan (Due Date) / Completion Date
#10 Community Outreach to Increase Access to Health Care	Serves to assist enrollment in Medi-Cal and Healthy Families (including continuing Medi-Cal benefits for families recently terminated from CalWORKs) and access to prenatal care for pregnant women.	DPSS		Yes	N/A								
10a. Community Based Outreach and Enrollment Services		DHS	Performance Incentives $4,937,500	Yes	N/A	Original 5-15-01 Amend. 6-19-01	Original 5-15-01 Amend. 6-19-01	Signed 10-01	N/A	9-01 to 6-30-03	9-04-01	Scheduled with Workgroup 5-02-02	Approved 2-29-02
10b. Prenatal Care		DHS	Performance Incentives $1.325 million	Yes	N/A	6-19-01	6-19-01	Pending	RFCP released 02-02	7-01 to 6-30-02	7-01	Presented to Workgroup 02-07-02	Submitted to CAO
10c. Outreach to Terminated CalWORKs		DPSS	None	Yes	Target 6-02	N/A	N/A	N/A	N/A	N/A	7-00	Pending	Corrections in progress
10d. Media Outreach		DPSS	Performance Incentives $1 million	No	N/A	Pending	Pending	N/A	Pending	N/A	Pending	Pending	Pending
10e. Improving Interdepartmental Capacity		DPSS	Performance Incentives $400,000	No	N/A	Pending	Pending	N/A	Pending	N/A	Pending	Pending	Pending
#11 Hotline to Resolve Health Care Access Issues	Expands the Hotline for health care issues dealing with Medi-Cal case problems, health care access. Extends hours of Hotline operation.	DPSS	None	Yes	In clearance Target 6-02	N/A	N/A	N/A	N/A	N/A	1-8-01	Pending	(4-8-01) Corrections in progress

Project	Summary	Lead Agency	Funding	Dir. Svc. Yes / No	Board Memo Date	Board Letter Approv. Date	Implem. Plan Approv. Date	MOU Approval Date / Lead Agency Contract	Contracts (Start and End Date)	Sub-Contract	Service Start Date	Immigrant Planning Guide	Evaluation Plan (Due Date) / Completion Date
#12 Health Care Transportation	Considers the need and availability for medical transportation for CalWORKs patients.	DPSS	None	No	3-6-01	N/A	N/A	N/A			9-19-00		(6-15-01)
#13 "Health First"	Screens all CalWORKs/Medi-Cal/Food Stamp applicants for potential linkage to healthcare programs. Disseminates "We've Got You Covered" booklet and posters.	DPSS	None	Yes	Completed clearance. Target 06-02	N/A	N/A	N/A	N/A	N/A	10-00	Pending	(3-5-01) Corrections in progress
#14 Transitional Support for Homeless CalWORKs Families	Provides relocation assistance of up to $1,500 to CalWORKs families leaving publicly funded transitional housing program. Subsidizes for up to 24 months those working families reestablishing after leaving a transitional housing program. Subsidizes employment for CalWORKs families leaving publicly funded transitional housing programs.	CDC		Yes	N/A								
14a. Relocation Grant for Homeless Families			Performance Incentives $1.35 million *	Yes	N/A	Pending	Pending	Pending	N /A	Pending	Pending	Pending	Pending
14b. Tenant-based Transitional Rental Assistance.	**DELETED**												
14c. Transitional Subsidized Employment for Homeless Families			None	Yes	N/A	Pending	Pending	Pending	N/A	Pending	Pending	Pending	Pending

Project	Summary	Lead Agency	Funding	Dir. Svc. Yes / No	Board Memo Date	Board Letter Approv. Date	Implem. Plan Approv. Date	MOU Approval Date / Lead Agency Contract	Contracts (Start and End Date)	Sub-Contract	Service Start Date	Immigrant Planning Guide	Evaluation Plan (Due Date) / Completion Date
#15 Emergency Assistance to Prevent Eviction	Assists in up to two months arrearages in rent payment to avoid eviction for CalWORKs families experiencing financial hardship. This is a once-in-a-lifetime benefit, not to exceed $1,500.	CDC	Performance Incentives $675,000 (Single Allocation disallowed by State)	Yes	N/A	Pending	Pending	Pending	N/A	Pending	Pending	Pending	Pending
#16 Housing Counseling / Training	Provides training for Eligibility and GAIN staff on common housing issues of CalWORKs families to enable them to provide training/counseling to participants.	DPSS	Single Allocation $500,000	Yes	Pending	N/A	N/A	Pending	N/A	Pending	Pending		Pending
#17 Community-Based Teen Services Program	Identifies and resolves problems facing teens with the goal in mind to avoid pregnancy, graduate from high school, read at grade level, and reject violence.	DPSS	Performance Incentives $17,852,105	Yes	N/A	4-00 11-13-01 Delegated Authority	4-00	N/A	12-01 to 7-03 Contract Sample Approved 11-13-01	N/A	1-30-02	Pending	Pending
#18 Services to Teens with Special Needs	Provides supportive services to teens with special needs. This includes Asian-Pacific Islander teens, American Indian teens, and teens with disabilities.	DPSS	Performance Incentives $2.5 million	Yes	N/A	4-00 11-13-01 Delegated Authority	4-00	N/A	01-02 to 7-03 Contract Sample Approved 11-13-01	N/A	2-15-02	Pending	Pending

Project	Summary	Lead Agency	Funding	Dir. Svc. Yes/No	Board Memo Date	Board Letter Approv. Date	Implem. Plan Approv. Date	MOU Approval Date / Lead Agency Contract	Contracts (Start and End Date)	Sub-Contract	Service Start Date	Immigrant Planning Guide	Evaluation Plan (Due Date) / Completion Date
#19 Services for Emancipated Foster Youth Who are Parents	Expands the current program concerning life skills and independent living provided to youths leaving foster care in order to accommodate those foster care youths who are parents.	DCFS	Performance Incentives $550,000	Yes	N/A	Pending	Pending	Pending	N/A	N/A	Pending	Pending	Pending
#20 Teen Passport to Success	Provides activities geared to teens and based upon the Job Club Passport to Success program. Education, employment, health, and five other areas will be covered.	DPSS	Single Allocation $743,000	Yes		03-02	N/A	N/A	Pending	N/A	Target Date 08-02	Pending	Pending
#21 Staff Development for Teen Services Providers	Provides training to providers of service to adolescents in the best youth development practices.	DHS	Performance Incentives $500,000	Yes	N/A	Pending	Pending	Pending	N/A	Pending	Pending	Pending	Pending
#22 Services to CalLEARN and Other Teen Parents	Extends the current CalLEARN program to allow the teens more time to secure employment or training and to assist them with educational challenges and career planning.	DPSS											
22a. Wrap Around CalLEARN (WACL)		DPSS	Single Allocation $600,000	No	11-29-00	N/A	N/A	N/A		N/A	11-29-00	1-01	Submitted 9-4-01

Project	Summary	Lead Agency	Funding	Dir. Svc. Yes / No	Board Memo Date	Board Letter Approv. Date	Implem. Plan Approv. Date	MOU Approval Date / Lead Agency Contract	Contracts (Start and End Date)	Sub-Contract	Service Start Date	Immigrant Planning Guide	Evaluation Plan (Due Date) / Completion Date
22b. Career Counselors to Work with CalLEARN and Other Teen Parents		DPSS	Performance Incentives $900,000 Single Allocation $900,000	No	N/A	Pending	Pending	N/A	N/A	N/A	Pending	Pending	Pending
#23 Youth Jobs	Provides paid work-based learning opportunities, career planning, and job placement for CalWORKs youths.	CSS	Performance Incentives $9,787,500	Yes	N/A	1st year 4-18-00; 2nd year 3-15-01; 3rd year in clearance	1st year 4-18-00; 2nd year 5-15-01; 3rd year in clearance	4-00	N/A	4-00 (7 of 7 sub-contracts have been approved)	7-01-00	Approved 6-00	(3-5-01) Submitted to CAO Approved
#24 Public Library Services for Children and Youth	Expands After-School Library Homework Assistance Centers and encourages the use of libraries for teens and children.	Public Library											
24a. Homework Center			Performance Incentives $300,000	Yes	N/A	Pending	Pending	N/A	Pending	N/A	Pending	Pending	Pending
24b. Teen Library Card Campaign			Performance Incentives $200,000	Yes	N/A	Pending	Pending	N/A	Pending	Pending	Pending	Pending	Pending
24c. Support Services for After-School Child Care Enrichment Centers			Single Allocation $127,000; $31,000 each year thereafter and Performance Incentives $21,000		N/A	Pending	Pending	Pending	Pending		Pending	Pending	Pending

Project	Summary	Lead Agency	Funding	Dir. Svc. Yes / No	Board Memo Date	Board Letter Approv. Date	Implem. Plan Approv. Date	MOU Approval Date / Lead Agency Contract	Contracts (Start and End Date)	Sub-Contract	Service Start Date	Immigrant Planning Guide	Evaluation Plan (Due Date) / Completion Date
#25 Operation READ	Provides after school reading tutoring to neglected, abused, and delinquent youths in the care of the county.	Probation	Performance Incentives $790,000	Yes	N/A	7-25-00	10-00	3-7-01	N/A	Completed 9-00	10-23-00	Completed 9-01	(3-5-01) Phase I Approved 6/04/01
#26 Safe Places	Provides safe places by community agencies, schools, churches, parks, etc., after school and on weekends, as well as safe passage to and from schools and other locations for children and youths.	LACOE	Performance Incentives $2.4 million	Yes	N/A	Pending	Pending		Pending	N/A at this time	Pending	Pending	Pending
#27 DART/ STOP for CalWORKs Families	Provides domestic violence response teams for use by LAPD, Sheriff's Dept., and local law enforcement.	CSS	Single Allocation $2.2 million	Yes	N/A	11-6-01	N/A	MOU signed 01-09-02	N/A	7-00 through 6-02 4 sub-contractors	1-9-02	Pending	Pending
#28 Domestic Violence Prevention	Researches methods to determine the signs of domestic violence risk and to educate welfare-to-work participants and teens in what to look for and what to do about it.	CSS		No	N/A	Pending	Pending	Pending	N/A	Pending	Pending	Pending	Pending
28a. Assessment Risk Tool for Domestic Violence		CSS	Single Allocation $50,000 one time cost										
28b. Research: What Works to Stop Domestic Violence Batterers in L.A. County		CSS	Performance Incentives $100,000 one time cost										

Project	Summary	Lead Agency	Funding	Dir. Svc. Yes / No	Board Memo Date	Board Letter Approv. Date	Implem. Plan Approv. Date	MOU Approval Date / Lead Agency Contract	Contracts (Start and End Date)	Sub-Contract	Service Start Date	Immigrant Planning Guide	Evaluation Plan (Due Date) / Completion Date
28c. Staff Development for Teen Services Providers		CSS	Performance Incentives $500,000										
#29 School-Based Probation Supervision	Provides a Juvenile Probation Officer on site at the school to supervise all of the Probationers in attendance. The JPO is able to interact with the juvenile, the school and the family.	Probation	Performance Incentives $2.564 million	Yes	N/A	3-7-00	3-00	1-30-01	N/A	N/A	3-20-00	Pending	Phase I Approved 6/04/01
#30 Support Group for the Families of Children Aged 11 - 18 on Probation	Organizes the families of 50 youths on probation into a mutual support group to benefit children and youth education as well as adult income and employment.	Probation	Performance Incentives $150,000	Yes	N/A	4-17-01	4-17-01	Pending	N/A	5-21-01	7-10-01	Pending	Phase I Approved 8-21-01
#31 Strategic Support for Child Care													
31a. Child Care for non-needy caregivers	Pays for child care for those children in the care of employed non-needy caregiver relatives not in receipt of CalWORKs for themselves.	DPSS	Performance Incentives $5,352,500	Yes	N/A	Pending	Pending	N/A	12-00	N/A	Pending	4-30-01	Pending
31b. Increase availability of child care	Increases availability of evening, night, and weekend child care.	CDC & DPSS	Performance Incentives $2.5 million	Yes	N/A	11-01	11-01	MOU amend. Pending			11-20-01	7-2-01	Pending

Project	Summary	Lead Agency	Funding	Dir. Svc. Yes / No	Board Memo Date	Board Letter Approv. Date	Implem. Plan Approv. Date	MOU Approval Date / Lead Agency Contract	Contracts (Start and End Date)	Sub-Contract	Service Start Date	Immigrant Planning Guide	Evaluation Plan (Due Date)/ Completion Date
#32 Federal Family Support Services Network	Supports 27 collaboratives formed to provide family support for: (1) enrichment activities for youth, (2) child care, (3) community safety, (4) job training and support, and 5) access to health care.	DPSS	Performance Incentives $4.5 million	Yes	N/A	Pending	Pending	Pending	Pending	N/A	Pending	Pending	Pending
#33 Family Preservation	Expands Family Preservation services (an alternative to placement for families where child abuse or neglect has been experienced) to additional geographical areas and to include services to probation youth, Asian/Pacific families, and American Indian families. Service will increase for deaf and medically fragile clients.	DCFS	Performance Incentives $8,927,500	Yes	N/A	1-30-01	1-30-01	02-13-02	N/A	N/A	7-1-01	Presented 8-29-01	(4-30-01) In revision 12-20-01
#34 Home Visitation Program	Provides for home visitations to monitor first pregnancy and new mothers in order to provide parenting and health education through the child's second birthday.	DHS		Yes									
34a. Nurse Home Visitation Program		DHS	Performance Incentives $3.750 million		N/A	Original 2-18-00 Amend. 3-18-01	Original 2-18-00 Amend. 3-18-01	4-6-01	N/A	N/A	2-18-00	Presented 8-29-01	Approved 6-04-01

Project	Summary	Lead Agency	Funding	Dir. Svc. Yes / No	Board Memo Date	Board Letter Approv. Date	Implem. Plan Approv. Date	MOU Approval Date / Lead Agency Contract	Contracts (Start and End Date)	Sub-Contract	Service Start Date	Immigrant Planning Guide	Evaluation Plan (Due Date) / Completion Date
34b. Home Visitation Program and Case Management, Implementation, and Evaluation of 2-6 Alternative Models		DHS	Performance Incentives $1.5 million		N/A	6-19-01	6-19-01	Signed 10-01	N/A	Pending	Pending	Approved Tentative Date for Workgroup after contracts approved	Pending
#35 Peer Self-Help Support Groups	Provides for peer participation in Self-Help Support Groups to modify behaviors.	DMH	Single Allocation $275,000 one time cost	Yes		Pending	N/A	Pending	N/A	Pending	Pending	Pending	Pending
#36 Support and Therapeutic Options Program (STOP)	Provides for peer participation in Self-Help Support Groups to modify behaviors.	DCFS	Eliminated. Funded by another source										
#37 School Attendance Areas	Utilizes elementary, middle, and high school attendance areas as the common geographic unit within a SPA for health and human services needs.	CAO (Urban Research Division)	Single Allocation $100,000 one time cost	No	Pending	N/A	N/A	Mou Signed 2-27-02	N/A	N/A	Non-Service Project 01-01		(6-15-01) Approved 12-03-01
#38 Multi-Disciplinary Family Inventory and Case Planning Teams	Provides multi-disciplinary teams (DPSS,DCFS, DHS, Probation Dept., DMH, LACOE / LAUSD) to identify the family's total needs in order to develop a case plan as needed.	DPSS	Single Allocation $7 million	Yes	LACOE 10-3-00 LAUSD Pending	LACOE 10-10-00 LAUSD Pending	Approved by DPSS 10-10-00	DHS, DMH, DCFS, Probation Pending	LACOE 10-10-00 to 6-30-03 LAUSD Pending	N/A	11-13-00	11-30-00	(3-5-01) Approved 10-01

Project	Summary	Lead Agency	Funding	Dir. Svc. Yes/No	Board Memo Date	Board Letter Approv. Date	Implem. Plan Approv. Date	MOU Approval Date / Lead Agency Contract	Contracts (Start and End Date)	Sub-Contract	Service Start Date	Immigrant Planning Guide	Evaluation Plan (Due Date) / Completion Date
#39 County Family Resource Centers (FRC)	Locates geographically-based FRCs in high-need School Attendance Areas, in order to serve families receiving services from at least three of the six co-located agencies (DPSS, DCFS, DHS, Probation, DMH, and the local schools).	DPSS	Single Allocation	Yes	Pending	N/A	N/A	New Directions DPSS, LASUD, PUSD, LACOE, LAUSD, LAHP Pending	Pending	N/A	Pending	Pending	Pending
39a. County Family Resource Centers		DPSS	Single Allocation $100,000										
39b. Deputy Probation Officers for Family Resource Centers		DPSS	Single Allocation $1.25 million										
#40 Data Partnerships for Children and Families	Establishes data-sharing across County departments and outside organizations for the purpose of making policy decisions and tracking program effectiveness. Provides for analysis of LTFSS needs and services.	CPC	Performance Incentives $575,000	No	N/A	12-18-01	12-18-01	N/A	12-18-01	N/A	12-18-01	Pending	Pending
#41 Service Planning Area Council Staff and Technical Assistance	Provides for additional professional staff support and technical assistance to the Service Planning Area Councils for their involvement with LTFSS.	CPC	Performance Incentives $637,000 per year for two years	No	N/A	4-18-00	4-18-00	N/A	7-1-00 to 6-30-02	11-00	07-01-00	Pending	(6-15-01) Phase I Approved 12-3-01

Project	Summary	Lead Agency	Funding	Dir. Svc. Yes / No	Board Memo Date	Board Letter Approv. Date	Implem. Plan Approv. Date	MOU Approval Date / Lead Agency Contract	Contracts (Start and End Date)	Sub-Contract	Service Start Date	Immigrant Planning Guide	Evaluation Plan (Due Date) / Completion Date
#42 CalWORKs Systems Review	Provides review, through an independent firm, of the linking systems and partner agencies involved with CalWORKs to determine their impact and effectiveness.	DPSS	Single Allocation $500,000 one time cost	No	Pending	N/A	N/A	N/A	N/A	N/A	11-8-01	Pending	Pending
#43 New Directions Long-Term Family Self-Sufficiency Committee	Comprises a committee of County department and agency representatives, as well as other community and public advocates, to assess implementation of LTFSS.	DPSS	None	No	N/A	N/A	N/A	New Directions	N/A	N/A	1-00	Approved 9-01	(6-15-01) Pending
#44 CalWORKs Case Management	Assesses the needs of CalWORKs participants and facilitates interaction between DPSS and outside service agencies.	DPSS	None	No	N/A	N/A	N/A	N/A	N/A	N/A	Partially Started 10-00	Approved 2-7-02	(6-15-01) Pending
#45 TranStar Enhancement	Provides a trip planning software system using landmark information such as child care centers and DPSS offices.	DPSS	Single Allocation $215,000 one time cost	No	NA	Pending	N/A	Pending	Pending	N/A	Pending	Pending	Pending
#46 Long-Term Family Self-Sufficiency Evaluation	Evaluates effectiveness of plan proposals.	CAO	Single Allocation $1 million and Performance Incentives $1 million	No	N/A	12-5-00	12-5-00	CAO	4-01	4-01	12-5-00	Approved 10-18-01	N/A

Some of this slow project rollout is a small project phenomenon. Fourteen of the 59 units (projects or subprojects) have total budgets of at least $2.5 million. Of them, 7 were delivering services by July 1, 2001. Of the remaining 7, 3 began delivering services since then; leaving only 4 (28 percent) that have not yet delivered services. In contrast, of the 45 units with total budgets of less than $2.5 million, only 19 have begun services, leaving 26 (59 percent) that have yet to begin delivering services.

This slow project rollout appears to have multiple causes. Part of the reason appears to be conventional problems with beginning new projects or, to a lesser extent, expanding existing projects—acquiring space, issuing Requests for Proposals (RFPs) and awarding contracts, negotiating interdepartmental and interagency memoranda of understanding (MOUs), hiring staff, and providing training. Given county procedures, these processes often take six months or more.

An additional reason, directly related to the LTFSS Plan structure, appears to be the multiple approvals required before projects could proceed—coordination between the lead County agency and DPSS and then approval by the Board. Because Performance Incentive Funds (PIF) flow through DPSS and are required to satisfy the regulations of the funding agency, the California Department of Social Services, DPSS required lead County agencies using PIF to clear their budgets and plans with DPSS. As we discuss in the next section, it appears to have taken DPSS about a year to provide guidance to lead County agencies about the coordination process and to put that coordination process into place. In addition, despite the fact that funds could not be spent until the Board approved the Implementation Plan, developing those plans required considerable senior staff time—for which new funds, and therefore new positions, were not yet available. In addition, this review process combined with DPSS leadership of the NDTF, and DPSS's need to obtain state approval for some LTFSS program activities (even after Board approval), caused some projects to view the LTFSS Plan as a DPSS effort, and that view appears to have influenced department buy-in.

In some cases, the LTFSS Plan service-integration strategy appears to have contributed to slow project rollout. Truly integrated service delivery requires close coordination between multiple departments in developing procedures and funding. Such integration requires more up-front planning, which takes time. In

- 78 -

some cases, problems reaching consensus on choices further slowed project rollout.

Even together, it does not appear that these reasons are a complete explanation for slow project rollout. Our interviews with participants in the process suggested variation in the priority assigned to the LTFSS projects on the part of the lead County agencies. In some departments, LTFSS Coordinators reported that they had trouble getting the attention of senior department staff or gaining sufficient resources to plan and implement their LTFSS projects.

The reason for this variation in priority given to LTFSS projects is unclear. In some cases, it appears that lead County agencies and project staff felt that the projects had been forced on them by outsiders involved in the open LTFSS planning process. In some cases, this resulted in their disagreeing with the basic program model or feeling that equivalent programs already existed. In some cases, lead County agencies were simply busy with a host of other tasks. As noted above, in the short-term, no additional staff was available. The slower rollout of smaller projects suggests that for some departments, the LTFSS projects may not have been large enough to warrant the management attention required to overcome the administrative hurdles. Finally, at least three departments—including DPSS—were undergoing major reorganizations during this period that also affected, for example, staffing of LTFSS projects. Rolling-out LTFSS Plan projects simply had to compete with other priorities, and the steps leading to project rollout were repeatedly pushed off of the active agenda for a variety of reasons.

Applying the Plan Is Problematic Given the County's Structure

By its charter and by its practices, the County has a Board, no elected executive, and strong departments that report directly to the Board. As a result, interdepartmental operations require interdepartmental negotiations between equals, often delaying or preventing the conclusion of the negotiations. The Board attempted to address this issue by delegating authority over and responsibility for the LTFSS to the NDTF—an interagency group. However, our interviews suggested that the NDTF was unable to prevent the LTFSS from being perceived as a DPSS effort, and that some interviewees interpreted that as being the Board's intention. Furthermore, the NDTF structure does not appear to have been sufficient to ameliorate interdepartmental coordination issues.

Thus, it remained true that interdepartmental operations were negotiations between equals. As a consequence, project rollout was often delayed by a drawn-out process of negotiating cooperative agreements, confirming that expenditure, scope of work, procedures, accounting systems, and protections of confidentiality were consistent with the requirements of the funding sources. However, the Plan does not account for this additional complication (e.g., by adding additional time and resources up front to plan for implementation before projects are expected to begin). The County also does not have procedures in place to prevent the entire effort from being perceived as one agency's agenda rather than as a cooperative effort as frustrations build over how to integrate services and how to set up mechanisms to move LTFSS funds across agencies. The need for additional planning time was discussed above; evidence from our interviews shows that to some extent the latter problem, that the Plan is seen as one agency's venture, has also been an issue.

To elucidate the issue, we turn first to the interagency structure of the County and then to how the Plan is managed by the agency tasked with oversight. Figure 6.1 shows that 11 different lead agencies are assigned responsibility for implementing specific LTFSS projects. The numbers in parentheses indicate the number of projects out of the total 46 that each lead agency is responsible for. DPSS has, in addition to its projects, a fiscal oversight role and the responsibility for coordinating the implementation of LTFSS projects. In this capacity, DPSS oversees and coordinates the review and clearance process for Board approval of projects' implementation plans and MOUs/contracts.

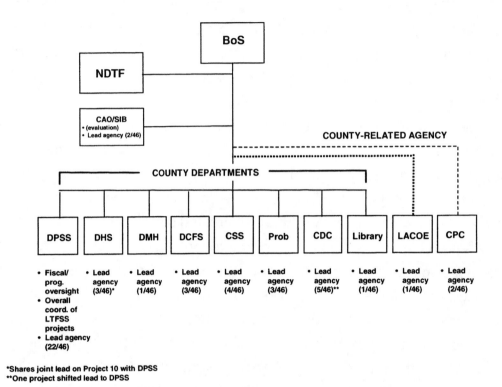

Figure 6.1—LTFSS Plan Organizational Structure

Overall oversight of the LTFSS projects' implementation was assigned to DPSS. The Board wanted one department to be accountable for how the money was being spent. As Chair of the NDTF, DPSS had led the initial development of the LTFSS Plan and administered the funding resulting from the CalWORKs legislation. Thus, it was DPSS to whom the Board would turn to if it felt a project was rolling out slowly and for an accounting of how the LTFSS Plan funds were spent.

The interagency structure of the County and the assignment of the oversight of the LTFSS Plan projects' implementation to DPSS had two major operational consequences for projects. The first is largely the result of the Plan's emphasis on collaboration, which takes time. Project rollout was slow as the departments—DPSS and the other lead agencies—first recognized that there were considerable formal coordination issues that needed to be worked out and then developed procedures to address them. These procedures, however, had to conform to DPSS's legal obligation to account for spending federal and state dollars, which meant that DPSS had a significant role in approving projects' implementation plans. This responsibility was not obvious at first to the other agencies. Thus, the second consequence was that although both the RBDM Framework and the Plan call for coordination and cooperation, DPSS came to be seen as dictating the terms of collaboration when it came to the details of implementation. This was largely the result of trying to implement the Plan within the existing County governmental structure.

The majority of project interviewees commented that it was not apparent at first that the lead agencies would have to follow DPSS's detailed requirements in developing their Board letters, line-item budgets, and other components of their implementation plans. One of the leaders in the earlier Countywide planning process commented that in retrospect, he/she would have involved DPSS contracts and fiscal staff earlier on during the planning process so that work could be started earlier on some of the administrative issues that would need to be addressed during the implementation phase.

Project interviewees also noted that the fiscal reporting and budgeting process was a challenge because each lead agency has its own set of guidelines and regulations to follow, with no standardized contracting or budgeting processes across County departments. Project interviewees also expressed frustration with the extensive review and clearance process, requiring input from a number of different entities within and external to DPSS. Many of the projects perceived that the detailed fiscal reporting and other requirements for the implementation plans were being imposed on them somewhat arbitrarily by DPSS. This led several of the project interviewees to comment that "this really was a DPSS initiative," in direct contradiction to the collaborative intentions of the Plan.

Frustration with the process of negotiating cross-agency contracts and financial reporting requirements was not one-sided. From DPSS's perspective, project staff did not understand that many of these requirements were set by the California Department of Social Services (CDSS) and Federal TANF regulations, not by DPSS per se. One non-DPSS interviewee thought that the lead County agencies had in some cases ignored the information provided by DPSS early on regarding the requirements for the different implementation documents. DPSS also found wide variation in the format and content of projects' draft implementation plans and other documents submitted for review. This led to DPSS holding a second Technical Advisory Workshop in April 2001 to provide projects with step-by-step guidelines on developing the different implementation documents and an overview of the review and clearance process for the implementation plans and for contracts and MOUs.

Once the LTFSS Plan Division was established within DPSS in January 2001, the project coordinators and liaisons also initiated one-on-one meetings with the individual projects, where the Division brought together all the relevant players within DPSS to work with the Lead County Agency on its implementation plans; this process helped to address many of the coordination issues. Indeed, these meetings were the ones most often cited by project interviewees as being particularly helpful. In general, the LTFSS Plan Division has been increasing the amount of technical support it provides to the projects.

These kinds of implementation challenges are directly related to the Plan's objective of coordinating services and programs across multiple agencies and to the LTFSS Plan's intent that PIF dollars would be used by multiple agencies to provide services to this population. Organizational differences in reporting processes and procedures must be addressed so that funds can flow across County departments and agencies, while also adhering to state and federal regulations and reporting requirements. This is a slow, difficult process in any coordinated service-delivery effort. However, it is even slower in the County because of the County's governmental structure, with departments that report directly to the Board. This structure reinforces the compartmentalization of different health and human services into different organizations. (Separate funding streams with separate reporting requirements have a similar effect.) In turn, this governmental structure may have contributed to the sense among interviewees that DPSS, in its position as "first among equals" in overseeing a multi-department effort, is imposing its will on the others. We note that this is a potential risk to any service-integration effort in the County, regardless of whether the oversight role falls to DPSS or to another agency. It is the governmental structure itself that makes the RBDM Framework difficult to implement in the County.

The LTFSS Plan Needs More Formal Links between Planning and Implementation

In a large county the size of Los Angeles County, those responsible for planning often differ from those implementing an initiative. This leaves room for differences in interpretation of the vision laid forth by the planners and the possibility of developing programs that may not be feasible or represent the best use of agency resources. Similarly, because the Plan lacks a mechanism for having implementers' input heard by planners, there is a risk that implementers will not be as invested in the product as the planners. We heard evidence of both outcomes with the LTFSS Plan.

Those who developed the LTFSS project proposals were not necessarily the same ones responsible for implementing the projects, leaving room for differences in interpreting the proposed projects. This frustrated some planners, who thought that their vision for the project was being altered; it also frustrated some implementers who thought that they did not necessarily have a good understanding of the planners' intent in designing a project. In addition, County staff charged with implementation thought that their expertise was being overlooked with regard to project content or how a project fit into the service-delivery system. As a result, projects can sometimes be perceived as imposed from outside the department. These tensions were apparent not only when planners were not County employees, and so were unfamiliar with County practices and capabilities, but also when representatives from one agency were planning for projects housed in another agency.

The RBDM Framework upon which the Plan is based notes that the entire process, from planning through implementation and evaluation, should be iterative, such that knowledge gained from experience in one phase feeds into the others. One of the suggestions that emerged from our interviews about the role of contract and fiscal gatekeepers in implementation was that future RBDM Framework planning efforts should consider including those gatekeepers in the discussion (in addition to service-delivery staff experienced with the subject area). It was thought that this would make the planners aware early on about the extent to which their proposals were feasible within the regulatory environment so that they could adapt their proposals accordingly. The flip side of adding implementers' voices to the planning discussion was adding planners' voices to implementation to ensure the continuity of their vision for the projects. It was thought that a mechanism for ensuring a continued discussion between planners and implementers as projects rolled out could increase the departments' sense of "ownership" of, and thus commitment to, the projects, and Workgroup oversight could ensure that their collaborative vision was realized.

Lack of Up-Front Planning Has Hindered Progress toward an Integrated Human Services Delivery System

Elsewhere in this chapter, we have discussed the progress the County has made toward service integration; specifically, we discussed that the planning process was more inclusive than has been true in the past, that it was driven by a focus on results and outcomes rather than on departmental priorities, that funding was shared across departments, and that some of the early difficult steps toward integration (reporting requirements, co-location issues, etc.) have been addressed. Nonetheless, one result of the various implementation challenges we have discussed in this chapter—the compressed planning time frame, the added complications of implementation given the County's governmental structure, the importance of ongoing communication between planners and implementers—has been a perception that the LTFSS Plan has not accomplished its strategy of integrating the human services delivery system.

Given the rapid pace of the Countywide planning process, the individual Workgroups had a limited amount of time to consider how the various projects might be related or could be restructured to fully integrate the various concepts. Those involved in the Workgroup planning process felt that the short planning time frame did not allow for full consideration of the Plan's service integration strategy. The RBDM Framework states as part of that process that it is important to "fit the pieces together" and to consider how proposed programs or approaches fit together into a system of services and supports, "not just a loose confederation of good ideas" (Friedman, 2001, section 2.12). The results of the planning process ideally should be vetted with the broader community.

Interviewees commented that there was little time to integrate proposals at the end of the Workgroup planning process. The Workgroups had been set up to address each of the outcome areas, with each group tasked to develop recommendations and proposals to address both programmatic and systemic problems in each area. However, as noted by five Workgroup participants and planning leaders, the short time frame within which they had to do this work left little time for cross-fertilization of ideas between Workgroups and to fully integrate similar concepts.

Interviewees from the Workgroup planning process also commented that there was little time to consider how to integrate LTFSS projects with existing service-delivery systems. Some observers were concerned that because LTFSS projects were overlaid on top of existing service delivery systems, LTFSS Plan services would not be completely integrated. They thought that having existing service providers more involved in planning would lead to fewer integration problems during implementation.

Planners were not the only ones concerned about projects being insufficiently integrated with the existing service-delivery system; implementers raised similar issues. In at least two instances, projects overlap with already existing programs, meaning that the implementers must determine how to ensure that these LTFSS projects complement rather than duplicate existing programs. Other interviewees raised the issue of LTFSS projects increasing referrals to existing service-delivery systems that already may be operating at capacity. They noted that the intent of a number of LTFSS projects is to improve the integration of the health and human services delivery system by being able to refer families to a range of programs within the County to more comprehensively address their service needs. However, some providers (e.g., substance abuse and mental health providers in some areas) are already dealing with a greater demand than there is a supply of services. Further, although referrals can be made to other programs within the County, it may still take a participant four to six weeks to get an appointment with a treatment provider or eligibility worker.

In future applications of the RBDM Framework, more planning time would help address some of these concerns. Of course, it is also the case that people have limited amounts of time and energy available for extended planning efforts, as well as competing demands on their time. In retrospect, many of the LTFSS planners believe that achieving the goals of the RBDM Framework planning process takes longer than six months, although how long the process should and could realistically take in Los Angeles County remains unknown. Finally, ongoing discussions between Workgroup planners and project implementers could also help in this area by anticipating service bottlenecks and by disseminating knowledge about existing services.

DISCUSSION

Two features of the planning process stand out as particularly noteworthy. First, as was intended by the Board when it directed the NDTF to think broadly about how to best serve low-income families in the County, many more individuals from various public and private organizations were involved in the planning process. Second, funding was spread across a number of departments and agencies to support projects. This is quite different from the usual method of retaining funding within a department. The LTFSS planning process was also viewed as the first Countywide test of applying the RBDM Framework to planning for health and human services delivery. The RBDM Framework appears to have been very useful in the planning process for the LTFSS Plan, particularly in the early stages of selecting outcome indicators and reaching a consensus on the main result the County wanted to achieve. Many participants commented that the LTFSS planning process represented an important step forward in terms of broad community involvement and a consensus-building, collaborative approach to planning. The planning process was considered a genuine attempt to involve all the relevant players (County and non-County). Despite the expressed concerns, most interviewed felt that the resulting process was more global and open than other planning efforts in the County.

Some of the issues that arose in using the RBDM Framework for the LTFSS Plan also point to how future applications of the RBDM Framework might benefit from the County's experience. In particular, planning participants felt the time frame allocated for this effort was short. Planning participants felt that more time would allow for even wider community involvement, more discussion of funding strategies to achieve the desired result of long-term family self-sufficiency, and more discussion of how to fit the pieces together at the end of the process—that is, to consider how the proposed projects might fit together into an integrated system of services and supports.

Other advantages accrue to longer planning and implementation time lines. The early stages of implementing a multi-department plan such as the LTFSS require time for management at three levels. First, procedures must be developed to facilitate communication and coordination across departments, agencies, and service providers. Second, more technical implementation issues must be addressed, such as how funding will flow across entities, what reporting requirements are to be put into place, and how projects will interact with each other and with the existing service delivery system. Third, the standard day-to-day implementation issues facing any new project must be tackled, such as site selection, staffing, training, and recruitment. It also takes time to involve community partners, to build trust, and to strengthen relationships.

7. ASSESSMENT OF THE EVALUATION FRAMEWORK

INTRODUCTION

Evaluation is a key component of the RBDM Framework because it generates estimates of the "results" that are then used to refine the implementation and to guide future project decisions and budgeting. As Friedman notes:

> Performance budgeting can present better choices by requiring each budget unit (internal and contract) to answer the basic questions in performance accountability: Who are your customers? How do you measure if your customers are better off? How do you measure if you're delivering service well?...These questions should be answered on a regular basis throughout the year, and used once a year to drive the budget (Friedman, 2001, section 3.16).

Consistent with this role of evaluation in the RBDM Framework, evaluation plays a prominent role in the LTFSS Plan, both in planning and in implementation. With some notable exceptions (e.g., the Manpower Demonstration Research Corporation's (MDRC) evaluations of the County's GAIN program), evaluation has not traditionally been a part of program rollout in the County. Thus, the fact that there is a strong evaluation component is itself a reflection of the positive effect of the RBDM Framework. Participants in the Countywide planning process and in the overall Evaluation Design Workgroup process stated that the RBDM Framework focused County departments and other key stakeholders on outcomes and on accountability. Furthermore, interviewees explained that the RBDM Framework and the materials produced by the CAO/SIB helped County departments to think more formally about program outcomes and has served as a useful framework for prioritizing departmental resources.

In this chapter, we provide an overview of evaluation process—developing a logic model, a list of headline and secondary performance measures, a data sources document, and so on. We then consider the extent to which those involved in the evaluation felt that the RBDM Framework was useful. We find, in general, that participants found the Evaluation Design component of the RBDM

Framework useful in principle in helping them think about client-level outcomes. However, most participants found it difficult to apply the Evaluation Design in practice. Of this group, some were simply confused about how to do the evaluation while others raised some methodological concerns about the Evaluation Design. The material for this chapter is drawn from Davis et al. (2001).

EVALUATION

In the previous chapter, we discussed the RBDM Framework in terms of planning and the Plan in terms of implementation. The final component of the RBDM Framework is a focus on evaluation through a particular evaluation model. We have already discussed some of the components of the RBDM Framework evaluation model in our discussion of planning. The core metaphor in the RBDM Framework approach to evaluation is a four-quadrant approach to program performance measures, with an emphasis on measuring outcomes in each of the quadrants. The quadrants are shown in Table 7.1.

Table 7.1
Four-Quadrant Schema

	Quantity	Quality
Input (Process or service delivered)/ Effort	Quadrant I How much service did we deliver?	Quadrant II How well did we deliver the service?
Output (Product of client condition achieved)/ Effect	Quadrant III How much effect/change did we produce?	Quadrant IV What quality of effect/change did we produce?

As specified in the County's LTFSS Evaluation Design, project-level evaluations are to include seven steps, as described below.

Logic Model. Each project is to specify the theoretical relationship between the project's intervention and the outcomes for children and families (i.e., Quadrant IV).

Performance Measures. Projects need to articulate goals, or performance measures, against which to evaluate their impact. Those performance measures should be both at the level of project actions (Quadrants I and II) and at the level of client effects (Quadrants III and IV).

Data Sources Document. Having identified the performance measures, the project then develops a document describing the sources and methods to be used to collect this data over time, both before and after project implementation. If historical data are not available, the project is to construct a comparable group who do not receive services to compare outcomes to project participants.

Progress Graph. From the identified data sources, the project should tabulate and plot the historical data for the headline performance measure. The project should then use the historical trend to develop a forecast of the future level of the headline indicator "in the absence of the project." As much as possible, the forecast should include information on other factors that may affect the headline performance measure.

Stories Behind the Baseline. A project then constructs a narrative discussing the factors likely to affect the baseline. What explains differences in outcomes that exist across subgroups? What contributed to the historical trend? What factors influenced the forecast's development? What factors may have influenced actual trends after program implementation? What differences exist between baseline and actual data trendlines, and why do they differ?

Identifying Partners. The RBDM Framework emphasizes that outcomes do not change because of government efforts alone. Each project is asked to identify other organizations—public and private partners—that have affected or could affect the outcomes of interest.

Quality Improvement Steps. Having considered outcomes to date, projects should consider what changes can be made to improve outcomes. This is the key step in continuous quality improvement.

UTILITY OF THE RBDM FRAMEWORK IN THE EVALUATION PROCESS

The LTFSS Plan Evaluation Design Helped Introduce Lead Agency Staff to the RBDM Framework

Under the clear influence of Friedman, the LTFSS Plan emphasizes the importance of focusing on outcomes and on measuring progress toward those goals. Consistent with the emphasis on outcomes, every project has been required to develop an evaluation that conforms to an explicitly specified version of the Friedman approach. A number of participants praised Friedman's model and its utility in terms of helping individuals at all levels to focus on client-level outcomes versus simply process measures. First, it is a noteworthy accomplishment that the model has served to guide County departments and agencies in thinking more formally about program outcomes. Second, it also has allowed them to focus on a common set of outcomes. Third, it also has provided a useful RBDM Framework for prioritizing departmental resources. Fourth, participants felt that the Friedman model has helped County departments and agencies to learn to "speak a common language" focused around strategic planning, outcomes, and evaluation. These were goals of the LTFSS Plan and are important steps toward the County's goal of stabilizing families by building their capacity to become self-sufficient.

Friedman's training sessions on the RBDM Framework were described by four interviewees as having made evaluation more accessible to senior managers and to nonresearch-trained staff. As one senior manager noted, "when Friedman spoke, it represented a complete turn around by senior management in that there was a sense of 'Now I get it. ...' An understanding that evaluation can be done by regular people was alone valuable." Another lead agency interviewee noted that evaluation is new to their project staff and Friedman's training sessions have helped them to think about evaluation in a more straightforward way.

Training on Applying the Evaluation Design Has Been Helpful, but Interviewees Feel More One-on-One Training Is Needed

In addition to the training by Friedman himself, the CAO/SIB has provided other training and technical assistance. In December 2000, the CAO/SIB held an all-day training session with over 100 County departmental representatives. The training was intended to provide them with an overview of the project evaluation implementation plan and to introduce them to the Evaluation Design itself and Friedman's approach. CAO/SIB prepared and distributed a detailed Project Evaluation Implementation Guide to help projects in developing project evaluation deliverables and to help project evaluators to implement the Countywide Evaluation Design and apply Friedman's results-based decisionmaking model.

In recognition of the challenges associated with developing the project evaluations, since July 2000, CAO/SIB also has provided one-on-one assistance to projects to help them develop their logic models, refine their performance measures, and work through the other evaluation deliverables. The CAO/SIB also is helping projects identify best-practice program models and models of change that might serve as a theoretical basis for their programs, as well as examples of programs that have been implemented. In addition, CAO/SIB is helping projects to identify appropriate comparison groups and data sources, and provide technical assistance to projects in the area of information systems development.

Project interviewees thought the consultation sessions provided them with a good introduction to the RBDM Framework and the LTFSS Plan Evaluation Design. However, the majority of the interviewees felt they needed more one-on-one assistance in developing their logic models and in working through the six steps of the projects evaluation development process. Project coordinators and program staff varied in the amount of training they had received because of turnover in projects or lead agency staff or because of schedule conflicts. As noted by CAO/SIB, for some of the earlier sessions, some projects were not far enough along to fully benefit from the training. Interviewees from one lead agency anticipated a future challenge as providing training for project contractors on the Evaluation Design to ensure that they implement it appropriately.

As noted above, the CAO/SIB developed a detailed implementation guide to assist projects in developing their evaluation deliverables and in applying Friedman's results-based decisionmaking model. The Results-Based Accountability Training Manual provides projects with step-by-step guidelines developed by the FPSI on results-based decisionmaking and budgeting, examples of program logic models to assist them in developing their own evaluation, and sources for additional references that explain the RBDM Framework and its application. In addition, the CAO/SIB meets at least quarterly with the Evaluation Design Workgroup. These meetings bring together representatives from all the lead County agencies. The Workgroup is charged with continuing to guide the design and implementation of the LTFSS Plan Evaluation and to oversee Countywide evaluation deliverables.[1] Interviewees indicated that these meetings also represent a chance to share progress on their

_____

[1]County of Los Angeles Long-Term Family Self-Sufficiency Plan Evaluation Design, page 3, October 23, 2000.

projects evaluation deliverables and to discuss problems encountered and how they are being addressed.

Projects Have Experienced Various Difficulties in Applying the Evaluation Design

While other evaluation approaches focus only on services delivered without considering their effect on outcomes, Friedman's approach emphasizes both outcomes and program measures. Involving project staff in the effort to measure services delivered and client-level outcomes is also important. Careful measurement—over a long period of time, with detail on geography and background characteristics—is the foundation of any evaluation effort.

The RBDM Framework is seen by many participants as valuable. Nevertheless, in our interviews, interviewees also raised concerns that the RBDM Framework was difficult to understand and difficult to implement. There was, therefore, concern that individual projects might implement the Framework differently. This difficulty was recognized early, as was evident in the early discussions of the Evaluation Design Workgroup. As summarized by several participants, the nature of those Workgroup discussions centered on how to apply the RBDM Framework and how to make it work. Their discussions included how to conceptualize the relationship between the individual project evaluations and that of the Plan as a whole, and the timing of the different elements of the Evaluation Design.

More generally, interviews with the Evaluation Design Panel members indicated three areas in which projects were having difficulty applying the evaluation component of the RBDM Framework: (1) logic models that were missing a theoretical basis or a model of change for the proposed project; (2) confusion about which quadrant a performance measure might fall in and, in some instances, duplication between the headline and secondary measures; and (3) the fact that a few projects identified a large number of performance measures per quadrant that the Panel felt was unrealistic.

As a result, a number of draft project evaluation deliverables submitted initially were returned to the lead agencies for revisions (with some requiring multiple revisions). The time line for when deliverables were due, in fact, was set up by the Workgroup when developing the Evaluation Design to allow for the early identification of problems that projects may be experiencing. As part of the review process, Panel members and the CAO/SIB provided a variety of suggestions to projects on how to strengthen their evaluation deliverables, including possible data sources, relevant comparison groups or historical controls, and additional performance measures to consider. Several interviewees stated that the Panel members thought it was important to address design problems early on rather than have projects implement flawed evaluations. This is consistent with the emphasis that the RBDM Framework places on evaluation. Evaluation Design Panel members also noted that projects are making progress in this area. In their view, projects appear to be improving in such areas as identifying appropriate performance measures in identifying a theoretical basis for their programs.

Interviewees commented that the Evaluation Design Workgroup meetings were only somewhat helpful to them in working through the development of their project evaluation deliverables. Several interviewees commented that staff turnover among the lead agencies has meant that issues discussed or decisions made in previous meetings had to be repeated with new project staff at subsequent meetings. They also commented that the individuals the lead agencies sent to these meetings varied in level of expertise (e.g., data staff and program staff), which led to some unevenness in the experience and focus of Workgroup discussions. Several interviewees felt that CAO/SIB staff clearly understood the evaluation concepts and RBDM Framework, but that they had not yet explained it well to the projects.

The CAO LTFSS Plan Evaluation project's budget includes a supplemental funding set-aside from which the lead agencies can request support for their project evaluations. Based on input from the lead agencies, the Evaluation Design Panel identified five priority areas for the use of these funds: (1) purchase computer hardware or software; (2) train staff on the use of statistical or database software; (3) hire evaluation or information science (IS) consultants; (4) cover evaluation reports' printing costs; and (5) pay for staff time to retrieve data from DPSS information systems.[2] Given the projects' slow rollout, project interviewees and CAO/SIB expect that the amount of supplemental funding requested for project evaluations will rise in the latter half of the current state

_____

[2]Memo entitled "LTFSS Plan Evaluation Supplemental Resources", sent to LTFSS Coordinators, from A. Drakodaidis, CAO/SIB, May 7, 2001.

fiscal year (FY) and the beginning of next FY (FY 2002–2003) as the evaluation-related technical assistance needs of lead agencies rise.

The projects' requests for supplemental funds to support the technological infrastructure required to track data do not solve all their data concerns. Members of the Evaluation Design Panel indicated that one of the major areas in which projects are having difficulties in applying the RBDM Framework is data-related. The Panel noted two key data-related issues: (1) difficulties in identifying historical control or comparison groups; and (2) difficulties in identifying data sources and a lack of knowledge about what data might be available. About half of project interviewees stated that they were not far enough along yet on their Evaluation Designs to address data-related issues. Still, a review of projects' draft Evaluation Designs and data sources documents indicates that projects have also recognized a number of data quality issues that may ultimately affect their ability to accurately measure performance measures and track service delivery.

Data issues may seem like minor technical issues, but the RBDM Framework places a great deal of emphasis on evaluation as part of its mandate to bring results-based accountability to service-delivery programs. It is useful as something other than a planning tool to the extent it is implementable, and the issue of data quality and availability (as well as the availability of skills to understand and interpret data, as we discuss below) thus speak directly to the utility of the RBDM Framework.

Not all data-related problems are directly RBDM Framework-related. Issues related to confidentiality restrictions, sharing of client information, and sharing of data (e.g., no consistent, unique identifiers across departmental databases) also have been experienced by the State and counties in the implementation of welfare reform and CalWORKs, as well as the LTFSS Plan (Klerman et al., 2001). Other problems are a direct implication of moving toward results-based accountability, not just in the County but across the country. Research on applying results-based decisionmaking and budgeting approaches indicates that an important challenge facing funders and administrators is establishing the infrastructure necessary to collect and analyze outcomes data (Liner et al., 2001). This is true not just for County entities but also for contractors and community participants. Outcome measurement is relatively new to many private nonprofit organizations, which are used to only monitoring and reporting such information as the number of clients served and the quantity of services, programs, or activities provided (Morley, Vinson, and Hatry, 2001).

Underlying these issues is the fact that evaluation or research expertise is uneven across the different projects and across County departments and lead agencies, something the Evaluation Design Panel called attention to. Several County departments have in-house research and evaluation units, whereas other departments do not. Project coordinators and program staff vary in the amount of education or formal training they may have had in research and in their experience in conducting evaluations. This variation has posed a challenge both in terms of developing the projects' evaluations and in recognizing the amount of technical support individual projects may require. This variation also potentially has implications for how well project evaluations may be carried out.

Finally, several interviewees noted that there was some ambivalence by the lead agencies about the value of the evaluation process itself. This is certainly not unique to the County. Research on results-based decisionmaking models and budgeting has found that one of the difficulties of implementing such models is overcoming staff and/or management fears about assigning blame if the results are not positive (Liner et al., 2001). Of course, the County's intent in adopting the RBDM Framework was to focus on measurable performance and accountability. With time, these fears may ease as comfort levels rise with familiarity; however, easing these fears also points to the need for ongoing education about the RBDM Framework and its purpose at all levels of organization, from management to line staff.

Projects Expressed Concern about the Ability of the Evaluation to Measure Program Impact

Interviewees also noted concerns that the Evaluation Design may not allow the lead County agencies ultimately to "prove effectiveness" or to measure "program impact." In measuring program effects and linking interventions to outcomes, a number of factors must be considered that may affect one's ability to measure causation, such as: (1) changes in the economic environment that may positively or negatively impact the outcome indicators of interest; (2) potential biases in the selection of program participants; (3) effects of other social programs on the outcome indicators of interest, making it difficult to identify the impact of a particular program (Rossi, Freeman, and Lipsey, 1999).

Recognizing this, interviewees commented that they thought the way a number of LTFSS projects were currently designed would make it impossible to evaluate their impact. For example, projects noted, as we discussed above, that incorporating economic conditions and other factors into the forecast of future trends is difficult.

The RBDM Framework acknowledges that evaluation is difficult. It warns against allowing the technical statistics to dominate the process but notes that "it can often help to have a statistical expert as part of the team" because the hard part about the baselines is the forecasting. "Turning the curve" analysis—changing an indicator's trend trajectory—is an important part of judging whether a program has been successful. The example provided in Friedman (Friedman, 2001, section 2.11) forecasts the number of vacant houses in a community, which was the indicator for the result "stable community with adequate housing." The forecast is generated by combining data on the trend in vacancies in the past, trends in local demographic change, and trends in economic conditions. Program success is judged by its ability to change the trend (e.g., in vacancies) against what that trend would have been in the absence of the program (e.g., the forecast).

A key element, then, is to correctly forecast future trends. Consider, for example, what the trend in vacancies would look like as the community entered a recession: Vacancies would most likely rise as residents moved out and new ones stopped moving in. Thus, a program that prevented the number of vacancies from rising could be considered a success in a recession; in other words, even if the number of vacancies remained constant, the program would be a success. However, if the forecast had not incorporated the effect of the economy on vacancies and instead had projected a flat or declining trend in vacancies, then the project would be judged a failure.

Programs in the LTFSS Plan face exactly this challenge—arguably with a higher level of difficulty—since it now appears that the economic expansion has ended and the County is entering into a recession of uncertain length and depth. It seems likely that such a recession will leave families with fewer resources and greater stress, which will appear in the data as downturns in many of the outcomes of interest. If the prediction of a recession and its negative effects on outcomes turns out to be correct, a simple pre/post evaluation (i.e., comparing outcomes after the change to outcomes before the change) or a comparison of outcomes with the pre-implementation time line that did not incorporate the effect of the economy would, therefore, conclude that the LTFSS Plan had had no effect.

In some interviews, it was difficult to tell if the underlying issue was confusion about the RBDM Framework itself, methodological concerns, or resistance to the idea of evaluation. For example, project interviewees questioned whether other evaluation designs might be better suited for individual projects and felt that there should be flexibility in projects' selecting what approach to use. Half of project interviewees, for example, felt the RBDM Framework was too rigid because the results had to fit into the four quadrants of the model and, thus, did not allow for measurement of other important information.

The RBDM Framework in fact anticipates some resistance. As it notes, "[t]he truth of the matter is that it is very rare to find an organization that 'wants' to do performance measurement. The reasons for this can range from organization inertia to fear about losing jobs, and everything in between" (Friedman, 2001, section 3.6). Friedman then specifies steps that organizations may take to address this, such as assigning a coach or more training to those who are resisting its use or demonstrating how the results of evaluation are practical and are used to affect decisionmaking.

That it can be difficult to distinguish confusion, concern, or resistance is evident in project evaluation deliverables that have identified (as required) a number of internal and external mediating factors that may affect the ability of a lead agency to measure a project's impact. These include the "buy-in" of the community; constraints imposed by shortages of services not in the projects' control, such as housing or child care; the willingness of participants to complete training or programs; and uneven knowledge across County departments' line staff about what programs are available, limiting referrals to needed services. These factors certainly can affect the ability of projects to achieve their goals, but some—like community buy-in or participants' willingness to complete a program—are within projects' ability to influence, and they should be expected to do so. The RBDM Framework notes that mediating factors in some circumstances can serve as a crutch:

[T]he point is that all programs' performance measures are affected by many factors beyond the particular program's control. This lack of control is usually used as an excuse for not doing performance measurement at all. Turnover rate, staff morale, you name it is "beyond my control." In fact, the more important the performance measure . . . the less control the program has over it. This is a paradox at the heart of doing performance measurement well. If control were the overriding criteria for performance measures then there would be no performance measures at all (Friedman, 2001, section 3.1).

Whatever its cause, projects appear to be frustrated with the evaluation component of the Friedman RBDM Framework. As one interviewee commented:

Although it is a useful planning tool at the strategic level, at the individual project level is where it appears to have been less well thought out. To answer the question "Are you better off now then you would have been?" is where things break down, because the tools to fully address that question have been less well developed.

As the RBDM Framework indicates, technical assistance and additional training may help clarify areas where projects are unclear about the purpose of the evaluation and about how to carry it out.

DISCUSSION

Project interviewees and those involved in developing the LTFSS Plan's Evaluation Design shared a similar set of concerns about the ability of lead agencies to measure program effects for the LTFSS projects. Interviewees with backgrounds in research or evaluation in particular questioned whether one could truly measure the impact of many LTFSS projects using the RBDM Framework.

Implementing the LTFSS Plan Evaluation Design (or evaluation in general) and the RBDM Framework's approach to evaluation is a difficult undertaking, and one that could benefit from considerable technical assistance. The consultation sessions offered to project staff to date have served to introduce lead agency staff to the LTFSS Plan Evaluation Design and RBDM Framework. While such sessions are arguably sufficient to allow project staff to understand the key ideas and to work with specialists, many of the comments suggest that the technical assistance received to date may not be sufficient to allow current project staff to develop, implement, and write up effective evaluations. Additional training could also serve to reduce resistance to evaluation, as the RBDM Framework itself points out. More specialized technical assistance may be needed to help projects address the real methodological issues they face in measuring the impact of their programs. Finally, an evaluation is only as strong as the data going into it. As projects move into data collection and analysis, additional technical assistance would be useful to help projects address the complex data issues they face in implementing evaluations of these types of programs—obtaining cross-agency data and upgrading computer software and hardware.

8. QUALITY IMPROVEMENT STEPS

INTRODUCTION

As of January 2002, almost three years after the initiation of the planning process and two years after the approval of the LTFSS Plan, about half the projects have begun to serve clients. This schedule is slower than had been expected, but in retrospect, implementation has proceeded about as fast as should have been expected. The LTFSS Plan is designed to achieve its desired result—long-term self-sufficiency for low-income families—by implementing projects developed around the RBDM Framework. The new model includes increased community involvement in planning, flowing funds across departments, and service integration. It is not surprising, then, that project rollout under this new, more complicated model is not complete. The history of the LTFSS Plan to date suggests promise. The County has shown that it can plan and implement according to this new model—"planning for results" as conceptualized by the RBDM Framework. As experience accumulates, refined procedures and processes should allow for improved Plan performance.

Thus, this is an appropriate time for the NDTF to consider what progress the Plan has made toward achieving its goal. Moreover, the County's financial picture has changed, bringing with it a reassessment of its spending, including for the LTFSS Plan. The Plan was conceived and executed at a time when there was considerable funding for the effort. A combination of federal funding through block grants with a State Maintenance of Effort requirement and rapid caseload decline resulted in generous funding for State and County welfare operations. The CalWORKs legislation also provided that all the savings resulting from any decline in aid payments were to be returned to the counties in the form of "Performance Incentive Payments." The robust economy and the rapidly dropping caseload led to the accumulation of such PIF monies well in excess of any initial expectation. By early 1999, the County had "earned" about $400 million in PIF monies (later raised to about $460 million). By January 2002, however, the State's and County's financial situations had changed because of the economic recession and declining business investment, especially in technology.

- 104 -

In light of this budgetary environment, we discuss in this chapter one issue for the New Directions Task Force to consider to bring about more progress in relation to the baseline indicators. This report has focused on the Countywide evaluation; correspondingly, the issue we raise here speaks to the overall effort, not to what any single project could do to improve its performance.

BUDGETING AND REBUDGETING

As the implementation of the LTFSS Plan moves into its third calendar year, lead agencies and LTFSS projects enter a new phase. From a management perspective, lead agencies will move from an emphasis on developing projects' implementation plans and putting an initial program in place to an emphasis on service delivery, refining LTFSS projects, overseeing contractors, and evaluating these projects and tracking outcomes. According to the RBDM Framework, the process is iterative. We are now well into the first cycle of planning, implementation, and evaluation. Lessons learned from implementation and evaluation should then cycle back into a follow-on planning phase. Based on those lessons, the RBDM Framework indicates that some projects would have their funding increased, some projects would have their funding decreased, some projects would be terminated, and some new projects would be initiated based on new or newly perceived needs and new program models developed elsewhere.

Implicit in the original funding for the projects is that this reevaluation would happen at the end of the five-year period covered by the Plan. However, California and the County face changes in their fiscal situation. As of January 2002, DPSS has reported a shortfall that could be as large as $70.4 million in the Single Allocation funding received from the State to sustain the welfare-to-work services of the CalWORKs program.[1] It is too early to predict what changes will be enacted, but funding is likely to be considerably tighter and there is discussion about using some of the LTFSS Plan funding for core WTW services.

Clearly, according to the RBDM Framework, these follow-on planning choices should be influenced by the accumulating evidence. Successful and fast implementation contributes to a case for continued and perhaps increased

---

[1]Agenda for the Regular Meeting of the Board of Supervisors, January 15, 2002.

funding. Similarly, RBDM Framework-based evaluation evidence of effectiveness should also contribute to a case for continued and perhaps increased funding. Finally, conventional research evidence of program efficacy and cost-effectiveness should also contribute to a case for continued and perhaps increased funding. Conversely, programs that had poor RBDM Framework-based evaluation outcomes, rolled out slowly, and had limited or negative research evidence from elsewhere should be at higher risk of lower funding or even termination. Projects that have not yet implemented may have more difficult program models, but slow rollout may also be evidence of low buy-in from the lead agency, which does not bode well for the project's long-term prospects.

Politically, these decisions are always difficult, as was evident during the planning process for the LTFSS Plan. Those developing the LTFSS Plan considered several options for assigning funding amounts to the projects to be put forth to the NDTF. One option was to recommend that only some of the proposed projects be funded, with the remaining projects to be funded in the future contingent on the State allocation of funds. However, we were told that leaders felt this option was politically unacceptable given that these projects had been developed through a consensus-building, collaborative process that involved a number of stakeholders and that represented an important step forward in planning for the County. The option chosen by the LTFSS planners was to fund all the projects but at reduced levels. This meant that the decision about which projects to fund would be based solely on estimated costs. This appears to be contrary to the RBDM Framework and the stated principals of the Plan, which call for using the best available evidence on efficacy and cost-effectiveness. Similarly, as the initial LTFSS budget allocations are adjusted and future allocations made, the RBDM Framework would imply placing more emphasis on considerations of program efficacy and cost-effectiveness.

CLOSING THOUGHTS

The RBDM Framework and the Plan are helping the County to promote self-sustaining employment, helping teens become self-sufficient; to support stable housing, ensuring access to health care and curbing violence; to promote youth literacy, building strong families; to integrate the human services-delivery system; and to fundamentally change how the County does business in providing services to children and families. The changed operating philosophy embodied in the LTFSS Plan itself has begun to stimulate real cultural change in the County and the lead agencies. In addition, the County and the projects have worked hard over the first two years of implementation to put procedures and infrastructure in place to deliver services to low-income families in the County. Nevertheless, few of the projects are yet providing services. Over the next year, lead agencies have an opportunity to show that they can begin to provide services and that their programs can contribute to the well-being of these families and can positively affect the outcomes of interest.

APPENDIX A. DATA SOURCES

A careful selection of data sources is essential to implement a successful evaluation of the LTFSS Plan. The data sources are of two types: surveys and administrative files. Scores of surveys have been conducted of Los Angeles County that contain some information pertinent to the proposed indicators. Similarly, scores of administrative files contain information pertinent to the proposed indicators. Nevertheless, there are relatively few data sources that have covered the County using a consistent measure for a long period of time at a low level of geography.

Some LTFSS Plan indictors can be measured from more than one source. When that is the case, each source has its own characteristics, such as available time lines, geography, and socioeconomic strata. Even the way in which an indicator is measured may differ significantly between two sources. As a general rule, we choose to use only the most powerful data source. This section describes our proposed data sources.

SURVEY DATA

Current Population Survey (CPS)

The CPS is a national household survey that includes roughly 130,000 individuals each month, and data for Los Angeles County are available beginning in at least 1977. The survey collects a variety of information pertaining to labor force outcomes for all people age 15 and older living in the household.

In each month, roughly 5,000 people in Los Angeles County are interviewed. Although the CPS samples are substantial, it may be necessary to merge two or more years of data to increase the precision of the estimates. In addition, the CPS is based on a clustered sample design. Therefore, the standard errors of the estimates must take this design effect into consideration.

Eight panels are used to rotate the sample each month. A sample unit is interviewed for four consecutive months and, then, after an eight-month rest period, for the same four months a year later. Each month a new panel of addresses, or one-eighth of the total sample, is introduced. Thus, in a particular month, one panel is being interviewed for the first time and one panel is being interviewed for the second through the eighth and final time.

Interviewers use laptop computers to administer the interview, asking questions as they appear on the screen and directly entering the responses obtained. The first and the fifth month-in-sample interviews are almost always conducted by an interviewer who visits the sample unit. Over 90 percent of month-in-sample two through four and six through eight interviews are conducted by telephone, either by the same interviewer or by an interviewer working at one of three centralized telephone interviewing centers.

The CPS data are widely used, their quality is very high, and they are the official source for income, poverty, and labor force statistics for the federal government. Moreover, the data can be used to make consistent comparison between Los Angeles County and several other geographic areas, including the rest of California and the rest of the nation.

A disadvantage is that it is not currently possible to examine geographic areas within Los Angeles County; only Countywide analyses are possible. We recommend that obtaining subcounty identifiers be placed on the Data Development Agenda. If the Bureau of the Census grants RAND permission, we could use the UCLA Census Research Data Center to analyze confidential data containing more detailed geographic identifiers. At the same time, given the size of the CPS samples and the clustered sampling design, the standard errors of estimates at the service planning area (SPA) or supervisorial district (SD) level may be too high even if one could obtain the geographic indicators needed to calculate such estimates. As suggested above, one way to offset these limitations, but perhaps not solve them, is to merge two or more years of data.

In most months, the CPS supplements its core set of questions. We propose to use a variety of these supplements. Each supplement is discussed in turn.

March Supplement to the CPS

The March Supplement to the CPS, which is sometimes referred to as the Annual Demographic Survey, is used to generate the annual population profile of the United States, reports on geographical mobility and educational attainment, and detailed analysis of money income and poverty status. The labor force and work experience data from this survey are used to profile the U.S. labor market and to make employment projections.

Most important for this project, the March Supplement contains information on income from all components, including welfare. Therefore, this data source will be used widely to examine indicators separately by CalWORKs status and by income. Individuals living in Los Angeles County can be identified in the March CPS beginning in at least 1977. In March 1998, information on 5,815 Angelenos was collected. Historically, roughly 5 percent of the population has participated in Aid to Families with Dependent Children/Temporary Assistance for Needy Families (AFDC/TANF), implying a sample size of 250 to 300 CalWORKs participants in each year. Merging two or more years of data will likely be necessary to increase the precision of estimates for CalWORKs participants.

Outgoing Rotation Groups (ORG) of the CPS

The ORG files include the answers to the basic questions asked for each of the 12 months, as well as a special set of questions about weekly versus hourly pay that is asked in the fourth and eighth month of survey participation. The questions are asked of the portion of the population that roughly corresponds to wage and salary workers. (Self-employed persons in incorporated businesses are excluded.) The annual sample size is about three times greater than that for any individual month. Therefore, in any given year, the number of Angelenos included in the survey is roughly 15,000. Individuals living in Los Angeles County can be identified in the ORGs beginning in 1989, and the latest data available are from 2000.

School Enrollment Supplement to the CPS

Since at least 1994, supplementary questions on school enrollment have been collected in the October round of the CPS. The information includes a detailed set of questions pertaining to school enrollment, including type of school, and school fees. We estimate that roughly 5,000 Angelenos were interviewed in this supplement in each year.

Voting and Registration Supplement to the CPS

Every other year since at least 1994, supplementary questions on voting and voter registration have been collected in the November round of the CPS.

This information includes whether each person in the household is registered to vote, whether they voted, and why they did not vote in the recent election. We estimate that roughly 5,000 Angelenos were interviewed in this supplement in each year.

American Housing Survey (AHS)

The AHS is conducted by the U.S. Census Bureau to obtain up-to-date housing statistics. The AHS obtains a wide array of information from occupants of homes, including income, detailed housing expenses, household composition, welfare participation, and race. Roughly 3,000 homes in Los Angeles County were interviewed in the years 1980, 1985, 1989, 1995, 1999. Smaller samples, roughly 1,000 homes, were interviewed in 1983, 1987, 1991, 1993, and 1997.

The AHS is described in more detail at http://www.census.gov/hhes/www/ahs.html.

Decennial Census

The decennial census in 1970, 1980, and 1990 can currently be used. The 2000 public use microdata are scheduled for release this summer. These data are the best for obtaining estimates of a variety of indicators for narrow geographic areas. However, their usefulness is limited because they are only available every ten years. Estimates from the censuses will in many cases supplement and validate estimates generated from the CPS, which are available on an annual or monthly basis.

Los Angeles County Health Survey (LACHS)

LACHS was conducted in 1997 and 1999 by the County's Department of Health Services. Plans are under way for a third survey to be conducted soon. The LACHS is the broadest single source of LTFSS Plan evaluation data because it has questions concerning all five outcome areas, and it is likely to have sample sizes sufficient to calculate reasonably precise estimates for each SPA and SD. The main questionnaire was completed by 8,003 adults in 1997, with 2,363 completing the parent supplement, which is the source of information on parent-child interaction.

A Hispanic-origin question by area is asked, followed by a race question with the following major categories (multiple answers are allowed): White, Black,

Asian/Pacific Islander, American Indian/Alaskan Native, and Other. There is a follow-up question to specify the origins of Asian/Pacific Islander respondents.

CalWORKs Transportation Needs Assessment Survey (CTNA)

CTNA was part of a multifaceted assessment of the transportation needs of Welfare-to-Work participants conducted in 2000 (Urban Research Division, 2000). The study includes focus groups on transportation. There are also neighborhood transportation deficiency analyses based on access to transit to available jobs for which participants might qualify. This is a very thorough and informative report on access to transportation in Los Angeles County. The major disadvantage of the CTNA for tracking indicators and generating forecasts is that the first survey was not done until 2000, and it is uncertain how often the survey will be repeated.

ADMINISTRATIVE FILES

The administrative files contain data of two types: (1) events that must be reported by law, such as births, deaths, or incidents of child abuse; and (2) records from program participation, such as persons enrolled in programs to treat mental illness or substance abuse. There are serious problems in determining the prevalence of a behavior in the general population, e.g., domestic violence or substance abuse, from program participation administrative files. Most important, not everyone who suffers from, for example, domestic violence or substance abuse, participates in assistance programs. Therefore, changes over time in the indicator can be attributable to changes in underlying prevalence in the general population or changes in program resources, participant recruitment, participant screening, or the composition of program participants. For this reason, we will minimize the use of program participation administrative records as a data source for the indicators. Even some of the administrative files based on mandatory reported events, such as child abuse and domestic violence, are sensitive to social and agency changes in detection, reporting, screening, and disposition standards.

California Birth Cohort Files

These files include all live births in California for a calendar year that have been "followed" for one year to determine how many of the infants survived and how many died within their first year of life. These files include infant death data from death certificates and fetal deaths of 20 weeks or more gestation for that year. The data files are available from the California Center for Health Statistics. RAND expects to receive confidential identifying information—name of child and mother—that will facilitate linking with the Medi-Cal Eligibility Determination System (MEDS) file.

California Birth Statistical Master File

These files include all live births in California for a calendar year. Information includes, among other things, the weight of the baby at birth, county of birth, zip code of mother's residence, and mother's education, age, race, and ethnicity. The data files are available from the California Center for Health Statistics. RAND expects to receive confidential identifying information—name of child and mother—that will facilitate linking with the MEDS file.

Medi-Cal Eligibility Data System

The MEDS is an individual-level database that contains information on all Medi-Cal-eligible persons in California. The MEDS contains indicators of the type of assistance, allowing identification of current and former CalWORKs participants. The confidential data, which RAND will attempt to use for the evaluation, includes names of the case (e.g., mother) and the children. Name and age will be crucial for linking these data with administrative files from other sources.

The MEDS file has a lag of a few months before new program participant data and changes in participant status are entered into the file. However, when the database is updated for this lag, it has been found to be good for matching purposes.[1] An alternative to MEDS is the County's own administrative files on CalWORKs participants. However, with the change to the new LEADER system, it is unclear whether the County data system can be used consistently over time. Furthermore, RAND has extensive expertise with the MEDS files that will be beneficial for the evaluation.

---

[1]This statement is based on a phone conversation with Paul Smilanich, Research Program Specialist, California Department of Social Services, June 4, 2001.

Los Angeles County Department of Children and Family Services (LAC DCFS)

The case management information systems of LAC DCFS provide data on child abuse and neglect, out-of-home placement, and family reunification. These data are indicators for safety and survival and social and emotional well-being outcome areas. Data since 1987 are available; however, there was a conversion to a new system in 1997, and data for 1987 through 1995 may require more time to obtain than other years. The department is developing census tract geocoding capabilities. At this time, however, aside from DCFS areas, only city and zip code geocodes are available. Individual identifiers in the DCFS case management system include name, birth date, and mother's maiden name.

California Department of Social Services (CDSS)

CDSS provides reports since 1990, which can be used for comparisons with the County on child abuse and neglect, out-of-home placement, and family reunification. Data are presented by race/ethnicity. County data are the lowest level of geography presented in reports. Individual identifiers in the CDSS case management system include name, birth date, and mother's maiden name; however, permission is needed to access this data.

While the birth and death files have almost 100 percent coverage, the incidence of child abuse and neglect is not as easily determined from administrative files. Trends in these numbers can be affected by shifts in public awareness and by social service activities that affect rates of detection, reporting, screening, investigation, and disposition.

Los Angeles County Probation Department (LAC PROB)

Case management files at LAC PROB contain data on status violations of juvenile probation, but they are not by specific violation in electronic files. Specific violations could not be tabulated without going through hard-copy folders. Electronic case data are archived after two years, and hard-copy folders are purged after five years. Race/ethnicity information is available. Individual identifiers in the PROB case management system include name, birth date, and mother's maiden name.

California Department of Justice (CDJ)

Administrative files from the CDJ contain data on arrests for youth violent crimes and domestic violence. State and county data are available, as are data for cities above 100,000 population and law enforcement jurisdictions. Data are available for race/ethnicity. Youth violent crime arrest data are available since 1990, and domestic violence arrest data are available since 1988. Individual identifiers are not available from CDJ, which only receives summary-level data from law enforcement jurisdictions.

California Department of Education (CDE)

Administrative files from the CDE provide information on elementary and secondary school students reading at grade level and on high school graduation. Data on students reading at grade level are available since 1998, and data on students graduating from high school are available since 1992. The educational data are available by race/ethnicity. The data are available at the County and by school attended. However, the school attended may not be the school closest to the student's home. There are not statewide files with individual identifiers for students graduating from high school. Individual identifiers in reading test files would include individual name and birth date; individual-level files are not readily available.

Table A.1 provides a summary of the availability of data for each of the 26 indicators.

Table A.1
Summary of Availability of Data for Each Indicator

Outcome Area/Indicator	Years of Data Currently Available	CalWORKs Participants	Former CalWORKs Participants	Income	Race/ Ethnicity	Language	Census Tract	Zip Code	SPA	SD	County	Rest of State	Nation
Good Health													
Access to health care				*Access to health care needs to be defined — Add to data development agenda*									
Infant mortality	65–97	M (90–97)	M (90–97)	N	Y	N	Y	Y	Y	Y	Y	Y	Y
Low birth weight births	60–99	M (90–99)	M (90–99)	N	Y	N	Y	Y	Y	Y	Y	Y	Y
Births to teens	60–99	M (90–99)	M (90–99)	N	Y	N	Y	Y	Y	Y	Y	Y	Y
Individuals without health insurance	80–00	Y	N	Y	Y	N	N	N	Y (97&99)	Y (97&99)	Y	Y	Y
Safety and Survival													
Domestic violence arrests	88–98	N	N	N	Y	N	N	N	N	N	Y	Y	N
Child placement in out-of-home care	87–99	N	N	Y	Y	Y	N	Y	N	N	Y	Y	Y
Juvenile probation violations	99–00	N	N	N	Y	N	N	Y	N	N	Y	N	N
Successful reunification				*Relatively little information — Add to the data development agenda*									
Youth arrests for violent crimes	90–99	N	N	N	N	N	N	N	N	N	Y	Y	N
Economic Well-Being													
Annual income under poverty level	77–99	Y	N	NA	Y	N	N	N	Y (97&99)	N	Y	Y	Y
Adults employed by quarter	77–00	Y	N	Y	Y	Y	N	Y	Y (97&99)	Y (97&99)	Y	Y	Y
Percent of family income used for housing	80,85,89,95,99	~Y	N	Y	Y	N	N	N	N	N	Y	N	Y
Access to transportation				*Relatively little information — Add to the data development agenda*									
Adults earning a living wage				*"Living wage" needs to be defined — Add to the data development agenda*									
Homeless within prior 24 months				*Little to no information — Add to the data development agenda*									
Social and Emotional Well-Being													
Personal behaviors harmful to self/others				*Little to no information — Add to the data development agenda*									
Substance abuse				*Little to no information — Add to the data development agenda*									
Child abuse and neglect	87–99	N	N	N	Y	N	N	N	N	N	Y	Y	Y
Access to quality child care				*Little to no information — Add to the data development agenda*									
Participation in community activities				*Little to no information — Add to the data development agenda*									
Voting and registering to vote	94, 96, 98, & 00	N	N	N	Y	N	N	N	N	N	Y	Y	Y
Parent-child time together				*Little to no information — Add to the data development agenda*									
Education and Workforce Readiness													
Adult educational attainment	77–00	Y	N	Y	Y	N	N	N	Y (97&99)	Y (97&99)	Y	Y	Y
Elem./sec. students reading at grade level	98–99	N	N	N	Y	Y	N	N	M	M	Y	Y	N
Teenage high school graduation	90–00	N	N	N	Y	N	N	N	M	Y	Y	Y	Y
Mother's educ. attainment at child's birth	60–99	M (90–99)	M (90–99)	N	Y	N	Y	Y	Y	N	Y	Y	Y
HS graduation for moms giving birth before HS graduation				*Little to no information — Add to the data development agenda*									
Adults in education/vocational education	94–98	N	N	N	Y	N	N	N	N	N	Y	Y	Y

(Under "Geographic Unit": Census Tract, Zip Code, SPA, SD, County, Rest of State, and Nation; "Rest of" spans State and Nation.)

Y=yes; N=no; M=maybe; NA=not applicable.
~ Available for recipients of Supplemental Security Insurance (SSI), AFDC/TANF, or other welfare.
Reports of availability of data by CalWORKs status, income, race/ethnicity, and language apply to countywide estimates.

APPENDIX B. DATA FOR INDICATORS

This appendix provides the estimates for each of the indicators not on the data development agenda, with one table devoted to each indicator. Estimates are reported for the period 1990–2000, when available. Estimates for earlier years are not reported even when they are available because of space constraints. The evaluation requires measuring the indicators for various subgroups (e.g., CalWORKS participants, people in poverty, etc.), and estimates for each of these groups, when available, are also contained in these tables.

Estimates are reported for SDs and SPAs for some indicators. In some cases, the individual data that were used to construct these estimates were only reported at the zip code or census tract level. Therefore, a crosswalk, which was developed by the Los Angeles County Department of Health Services, was used to map the zip code and census tract data into SDs and SPAs.

Table B.1 Infant Mortality

Operational Definition: Number of babies born alive each year who die within 12 months of birth per 1,000 live births in that year.

	1990	1991	1992	1993	1994	1995	1996	1997	1998	1999	2000
Los Angeles County											
Countywide	8.0	7.7	7.4	7.2	7.0	6.7	5.9	5.9			
Race/Ethnicity											
Hispanic	7.2	6.9	6.9	6.3	6.2	6.0	5.4	5.7			
White, non-Hispanic	6.8	6.6	5.9	5.9	5.8	5.5	5.0	4.4			
Black, non-Hispanic	16.0	16.4	15.2	15.9	16.3	14.4	12.8	12.2			
Asian, non-Hispanic	5.7	5.8	5.2	6.3	4.8	5.1	4.9	4.5			
Supervisory Districts											
SD-1	7.2	7.4	6.6	6.4	6.1	6.3	5.9	5.9			
SD-2	10.0	9.6	9.7	9.3	9.1	7.6	7.5	7.4			
SD-3	6.6	6.9	6.2	6.1	6.3	6.0	4.8	5.5			
SD-4	7.9	6.8	6.8	7.2	6.7	7.0	5.2	5.3			
SD-5	7.0	6.9	6.7	6.3	6.0	6.1	5.6	5.2			
Service Planning Areas											
Antelope Valley (1)	9.6	9.9	8.7	8.2	8.8	7.5	5.6	9.0			
San Fernando Valley (2)	6.7	6.5	6.5	5.9	6.3	5.8	4.9	4.8			
San Gabriel Valley (3)	7.6	7.0	6.3	6.4	5.7	6.4	5.9	5.6			
Metro (4)	6.6	8.0	6.6	6.1	6.9	6.3	5.4	5.8			
West (5)	6.0	6.7	7.4	5.9	5.4	5.6	4.5	4.0			
South (6)	11.2	10.8	10.9	10.2	9.6	8.2	8.2	8.3			
East (7)	6.6	6.6	7.0	6.9	6.3	6.2	5.9	5.8			
South Bay (8)	8.8	7.2	6.6	8.0	7.4	7.5	6.0	5.8			
Rest of California											
All	7.9	7.3	6.8	6.7	6.9	6.2	5.8	6.0			
Race/Ethnicity											
Hispanic	7.4	7.2	6.1	6.3	6.5	6.0	5.6	5.6			
White, non-Hispanic	7.2	6.6	6.2	6.1	6.5	5.6	5.3	5.5			
Black, non-Hispanic	16.0	14.6	15.9	14.4	14.2	12.8	12.0	13.9			
Asian, non-Hispanic	6.8	5.7	5.9	5.3	5.9	5.0	4.8	4.8			
Rest of USA											
All	9.2	8.9	8.5	8.4	8.0	7.6	7.3	7.2	7.2		
Race											
White	7.6	7.3	6.9	6.8	6.6	6.3	6.1	6.0			
Black	18.0	17.6	16.8	16.5	15.8	15.1	14.7	14.2			

Table B.2 Low Birth Weight Births

Operational Definition: Number of babies born alive each year who weigh less than 2,500 grams per 1,000 live births per year.

	1990	1991	1992	1993	1994	1995	1996	1997	1998	1999	2000
Los Angeles County											
Countywide	6.1	6.1	6.1	6.2	6.4	6.4	6.4	6.5	6.6	6.6	6.4
Race/Ethnicity											
Hispanic	5.1	5.1	5.3	5.4	5.5	5.6	5.5	5.7	5.7	5.7	5.6
White, non-Hispanic	5.2	5.3	5.4	5.6	5.8	6.1	6.2	6.0	6.3	6.3	6.8
Black, non-Hispanic	13.0	13.0	12.9	12.5	13.0	12.7	12.3	12.3	12.2	12.5	12.0
Asian, non-Hispanic	5.6	6.1	6.0	5.9	6.4	6.4	6.8	6.9	7.1	6.8	6.7
Supervisory Districts											
SD-1	5.4	5.2	5.5	5.7	6.0	6.0	5.8	6.0	6.1	5.9	6.1
SD-2	7.5	7.5	7.3	7.2	7.3	7.3	7.3	7.4	7.5	7.3	7.2
SD-3	5.6	5.5	6.0	5.7	6.0	6.1	6.0	6.1	6.5	6.3	6.0
SD-4	5.6	5.6	5.6	5.8	5.9	6.1	6.3	6.3	6.2	6.5	6.1
SD-5	5.3	5.5	5.6	5.8	6.1	6.3	6.1	6.4	6.5	6.6	6.5
Service Planning Areas											
Antelope Valley (1)	5.2	5.4	5.6	6.0	7.0	7.2	6.3	7.2	6.8	7.8	7.2
San Fernando Valley (2)	5.4	5.3	5.7	5.6	5.8	5.9	5.7	6.0	6.3	6.2	5.9
San Gabriel Valley (3)	5.6	5.5	5.7	6.0	6.0	6.1	6.1	6.2	6.3	6.1	6.3
Metro (4)	5.8	5.8	6.2	6.0	6.3	6.7	6.3	6.3	6.8	6.4	6.3
West (5)	5.4	5.7	6.3	5.9	6.7	6.0	6.4	6.6	6.9	6.7	6.8
South (6)	8.1	8.0	7.9	7.6	7.6	7.7	7.8	7.8	7.9	7.9	7.5
East (7)	4.9	5.0	5.0	5.3	5.7	5.5	5.7	5.8	5.6	5.9	5.7
South Bay (8)	6.4	6.4	6.0	6.3	6.4	6.8	6.7	6.7	6.5	6.8	6.7
Rest of California											
All	5.7	5.7	5.8	5.9	6.1	5.9	5.9	6.0	6.1	5.9	6.1
Race/Ethnicity											
Hispanic	5.3	5.3	5.3	5.5	5.5	5.4	5.4	5.5	5.5	5.4	5.6
White, non-Hispanic	5.0	5.0	5.1	5.2	5.5	5.4	5.4	5.4	5.6	5.4	5.6
Black, non-Hispanic	12.2	12.5	12.6	12.9	12.3	11.7	11.7	12.0	11.4	11.4	11.5
Asian, non-Hispanic	6.2	6.4	6.4	6.1	6.5	6.4	6.7	6.8	6.9	6.9	7.1
USA											
All	7.0	7.1	7.1	7.2	7.3	7.3	7.4	7.5	7.6	7.6	
Race/Ethnicity											
Hispanic	6.1	6.1	6.1	6.2	6.2	6.3	6.3	6.4	6.4	6.4	
White, non-Hispanic	5.6	5.7	5.7	5.9	6.1	6.2	6.4	6.5	6.6	6.6	
Black, non-Hispanic	13.3	13.6	13.4	13.4	13.3	13.2	13.1	13.1	13.2	13.2	
Asian											

Table B.3 Birth to Teens

Operational Definition: Number of live births to girls 10–17 per 1,000 girls 10–17. For the USA, the estimates are reported for girls 15–17 years old.

	1990	1991	1992	1993	1994	1995	1996	1997	1998	1999	2000
Los Angeles County											
Countywide		20.7	20.0	19.6	19.3	18.7	16.9	15.2	13.8	12.5	
Race/Ethnicity											
Hispanic		30.0	29.8	29.2	28.8	28.3	25.7	23.5	20.9	19.2	
White, non-Hispanic		7.8	6.5	6.1	5.8	5.5	4.6	3.6	3.4	2.8	
Black, non-Hispanic		26.4	24.7	23.8	23.2	20.9	18.4	15.9	14.7	12.4	
Asian, non-Hispanic		3.4	2.9	3.0	3.1	2.9	2.6	2.6	2.5	2.2	
Supervisory Districts											
SD-1		23.6	23.5	22.7	22.2	21.6	19.7	18.3	17.1	15.1	
SD-2		29.0	27.4	26.7	25.3	24.3	21.0	19.1	17.3	16.2	
SD-3		15.1	14.9	13.8	13.4	13.0	12.5	11.3	10.6	9.4	
SD-4		16.9	14.8	14.9	14.8	14.1	13.1	12.2	10.9	9.9	
SD-5		10.2	10.1	9.4	10.0	9.4	8.7	7.8	7.1	6.9	
Service Planning Areas											
Antelope Valley (1)		16.5	14.1	14.2	16.0	15.4	14.0	13.5	12.9	12.2	
San Fernando Valley (2)		13.5	13.3	12.2	12.3	11.6	11.3	10.3	9.2	8.7	
San Gabriel Valley (3)		14.8	15.0	14.6	14.8	14.6	12.8	11.6	10.8	9.9	
Metro (4)		23.7	24.0	21.9	20.8	20.7	17.6	17.0	16.4	14.0	
West (5)		8.0	7.5	6.3	5.9	6.5	6.0	5.0	4.3	4.2	
South (6)		36.3	34.4	33.2	31.4	29.0	25.8	23.4	21.3	20.6	
East (7)		20.3	19.1	19.2	19.2	18.2	17.4	16.0	14.6	12.9	
South Bay (8)		18.6	16.2	16.7	15.8	15.5	14.0	12.5	11.1	9.8	
Rest of California											
All		16.1	16.0	16.0	15.8	15.1	13.8	12.9	11.8	10.8	
Hispanic		29.7	30.2	31.0	31.6	30.5	28.8	27.1	24.8	23.3	
White, non-Hispanic		8.6	8.2	7.9	7.5	7.0	6.0	5.4	5.0	4.2	
Black, non-Hispanic		29.5	28.6	27.2	24.8	24.8	21.0	19.5	16.2	14.4	
Asian, non-Hispanic		9.2	8.9	8.5	8.6	8.0	7.1	6.5	5.7	5.1	
USA											
All	37.5	38.7	37.8	37.8	37.6	36.0	33.8	32.1	30.4	28.7	
Hispanic	65.9	70.6	71.4	71.7	74.0	72.9	69.0	66.3	62.3	61.3	
White, non-Hispanic	23.2	23.6	22.7	22.7	22.8	22.0	20.6	19.4	18.4	17.1	
Black, non-Hispanic	84.9	86.7	83.9	82.5	78.6	72.1	66.6	62.6	58.8	53.7	
Asian	16.0	16.1	15.2	16.0	16.1	15.4	14.9	14.3	13.8	12.3	

Table B.4 Individuals without Health Insurance

Operational Definition: Percentage of people without health insurance.

	1990	1991	1992	1993	1994	1995	1996	1997	1998	1999	2000
Los Angeles County											
Countywide	26.2	26.2	26.9	26.1	29.1	28.9	27.5	29.1	30.1	28.7	23.1
CalWORKs/TANF/AFDC Status											
Not Enrolled	27.6	27.8	28.8	28.2	31.8	31.0	29.3	30.9	31.1	29.9	24.0
Enrolled	2.0	2.2	2.5	4.1	2.1	5.4	2.4	3.0	4.2	5.0	2.7
Below Poverty Level	46.5	46.9	43.2	44.3	43.6	40.0	40.6	39.7	48.1	45.6	38.0
Race/Ethnicity											
Hispanic	42.6	41.6	42.8	37.1	40.8	39.9	38.4	43.1	43.4	41.1	35.9
White, non-Hispanic	13.7	13.7	13.5	14.0	15.2	16.7	14.3	12.2	13.9	13.7	10.0
Black, non-Hispanic	16.5	18.1	18.1	22.5	21.7	25.2	20.5	17.5	19.0	21.0	13.7
Asian, non-Hispanic	22.1	22.4	23.6	25.4	35.6	25.5	30.4	30.8	34.3	31.2	22.0
Rest of California											
All	16.1	15.4	16.0	17.1	17.8	17.0	17.0	18.3	18.9	17.1	16.0
CalWORKs/TANF/AFDC Status											
Not Enrolled	17.0	16.4	16.9	18.2	19.0	18.0	17.9	19.1	19.6	17.7	16.6
Enrolled	2.1	1.1	2.6	1.2	1.0	2.1	1.9	2.8	2.4	1.6	0.3
Below Poverty Level	31.7	29.7	31.8	33.8	32.4	32.4	31.1	32.8	33.0	34.7	32.7
Race/Ethnicity											
Hispanic	32.0	28.5	30.0	27.5	30.3	32.0	29.0	30.6	34.7	29.2	29.5
White, non-Hispanic	11.2	11.0	11.4	12.6	12.7	11.5	11.5	13.1	12.6	11.1	9.9
Black, non-Hispanic	16.8	15.8	15.2	17.4	17.6	16.6	21.5	17.3	21.7	20.8	13.2
Asian, non-Hispanic	15.7	15.2	15.1	17.7	16.4	14.7	19.4	19.7	15.9	17.4	14.1
Rest of USA											
All	13.5	13.6	14.3	14.9	14.6	14.8	15.2	15.7	15.8	15.1	13.7
CalWORKs/TANF/AFDC Status											
Not Enrolled	14.1	14.3	14.9	15.6	15.3	15.5	15.7	16.1	16.2	15.4	13.9
Enrolled	2.0	1.6	2.1	1.9	2.0	1.5	2.2	1.9	2.2	2.1	1.2
Below Poverty Level	27.8	27.6	27.6	28.3	28.2	29.6	30.4	31.2	31.8	31.8	
Race/Ethnicity											
Hispanic	30.5	29.5	30.5	30.5	32.4	32.1	32.8	32.7	34.1	32.2	31.4
White, non-Hispanic	10.7	10.7	11.4	11.9	11.5	11.4	11.5	12.0	11.8	11.0	9.7
Black, non-Hispanic	19.8	20.7	20.1	20.3	19.5	20.7	21.6	21.2	22.0	21.0	18.3
Asian, non-Hispanic	16.1	17.5	19.1	19.6	18.1	19.5	19.9	19.4	19.0	19.7	17.2

Table B.5 Domestic Violence Arrests

Operational Definition: Arrests for domestic violence per 100,000 population per year.

	1990	1991	1992	1993	1994	1995	1996	1997	1998	1999	2000
Los Angeles County Countywide	251.2	250.3	261.3	249.5	266.3	274.4	271.6	276.7	252.1	229.2	211.7
Rest of California All	176.0	184.1	199.4	211.3	239.4	254.5	250.2	265.1	230.0	206.5	203.6
Rest of USA All											

Table B.6 Child Placement in Out-of-Home Care

Operational Definition: Children placed in out-of-home care during the year per 1,000 persons under the age of 18. Out-of-home care refers to living outside of the home of the parent or related caretaker.

	1990	1991	1992	1993	1994	1995	1996	1997	1998	1999	2000
Los Angeles County											
Countywide	4.6	4.4	4.4	4.8	4.5	4.5	5.2	4.7	3.4	3.2	
Rest of California											
All	3.2	2.9	2.8	2.8	3.1	3.0	3.1	3.5	3.9	3.6	

Table B.7 Youth Arrests for Violent Crimes

Operational Definition: Youth arrests per 100,000 youths per year for homicide, forcible rape, robbery, aggravated assault, or kidnapping. Youths are persons under the age of 18. These arrests do not necessarily result in complaint filings and convictions; these events happen after the arrests, and data on them are not available.

	1990	1991	1992	1993	1994	1995	1996	1997	1998	1999	2000
Los Angeles County											
Countywide	1064.8	949.2	913.0	817.9	773.0	772.8	724.3	646.5	590.8	535.6	
Rest of California											
All	479.6	533.6	544.4	560.4	594.4	565.2	544.0	518.4	500.4	476.4	
Rest of USA											
All											

Table B.8 Homicide Rate

Operational Definition: Number of homicides per 100,000 persons in that year.

	1990	1991	1992	1993	1994	1995	1996	1997	1998	1999	2000
Los Angeles County											
Countywide	21.4	22.5	22.8	22.0	19.4	18.8	15.8	13.4	10.6	9.5	
Race/Ethnicity											
Hispanic	19.3	19.6	18.3	19.7	16.7	13.4	11.7	9.8	7.4	6.7	
White, non-Hispanic	8.5	8.4	8.3	8.1	6.8	6.8	6.2	5.5	4.6	3.3	
Black, non-Hispanic	92.4	97.4	109.1	95.6	88.8	94.6	76.1	65.3	51.8	47.9	
Asian, non-Hispanic	6.6	11.7	8.1	9.2	6.4	7.9	6.5	4.1	3.7	4.2	
Supervisory Districts											
SD-1	22.5	22.1	24.9	21.4	21.7	23.3	16.1	15.0	11.6	10.3	
SD-2	46.8	47.0	50.5	49.0	44.3	37.9	34.6	25.9	20.8	19.4	
SD-3	11.9	13.1	11.9	12.3	8.8	9.9	7.1	8.0	6.2	5.2	
SD-4	13.8	15.6	14.6	14.7	12.4	13.0	12.1	10.9	9.4	7.6	
SD-5	6.3	9.3	8.7	9.9	7.2	8.2	8.1	5.7	4.5	4.4	
Service Planning Areas											
Antelope Valley (1)	6.2	11.2	12.4	9.8	12.5	11.8	11.8	8.5	7.3	5.2	
San Fernando Valley (2)	8.7	12.1	10.4	10.4	7.0	8.3	7.1	6.7	5.6	5.2	
San Gabriel Valley (3)	11.3	11.9	13.4	13.7	12.1	13.2	9.4	8.4	6.6	6.5	
Metro (4)	26.6	26.6	30.6	25.7	21.1	24.4	18.0	16.0	9.9	9.5	
West (5)	9.3	9.3	9.7	11.7	9.0	7.3	8.8	5.4	4.9	3.3	
South (6)	69.0	66.7	72.3	72.5	65.3	55.1	49.5	36.1	29.2	30.0	
East (7)	15.6	19.3	16.4	14.4	16.1	17.6	14.5	12.8	11.5	8.6	
South Bay (8)	19.6	19.6	19.6	20.2	17.8	15.7	14.3	13.7	11.6	8.6	
Rest of California*											
All	12.4	13.4	13.4	13.6	12.3	11.3	9.4	8.6	7.2		
Rest of USA*											
All	9.9	10.4	9.9	9.9	9.4	8.6	7.8	7.3	6.6		

* Source=CDC WONDER.

Table B.9 Adults Employed

Operational Definition: Percentage of adults 18–61 who were employed at any time during the year.

	1990	1991	1992	1993	1994	1995	1996	1997	1998	1999	2000
Los Angeles County											
Countywide	78.2	76.2	74.9	72.5	73.9	74.0	74.5	76.3	76.9	77.5	79.2
CalWORKs/TANF/AFDC Status											
Not Enrolled	79.8	78.9	77.1	75.4	76.8	76.8	76.6	78.1	77.8	78.7	80.1
Enrolled	27.8	11.9	20.7	21.1	23.0	20.4	22.6	24.6	36.7	32.5	43.0
Below Poverty Level	48.1	43.0	43.7	41.9	40.1	43.2	43.5	42.5	47.2	45.6	44.5
Race/Ethnicity											
Hispanic	73.5	71.2	69.4	68.6	68.8	70.9	73.6	71.3	73.3	74.8	75.4
White, non-Hispanic	83.0	81.4	80.2	79.3	80.6	80.8	79.9	84.3	83.4	82.1	85.2
Black, non-Hispanic	76.1	71.3	68.6	66.5	74.3	66.4	68.2	72.4	75.4	74.2	79.7
Asian, non-Hispanic	77.9	78.3	77.9	68.6	69.6	70.4	67.9	74.4	72.5	75.6	74.4
Rest of California											
All	81.1	80.6	79.5	79.3	80.5	79.6	80.2	80.7	80.3	80.6	81.3
CalWORKs/TANF/AFDC Status											
Not Enrolled	83.0	82.6	81.7	81.3	82.5	81.6	81.9	81.7	81.1	81.1	81.9
Enrolled	34.3	30.7	31.7	34.3	35.5	31.8	32.3	47.6	49.0	58.6	50.7
Below Poverty Level	47.0	50.0	47.0	48.2	45.1	45.7	47.5	50.1	46.2	49.9	51.6
Race/Ethnicity											
Hispanic	77.1	74.8	75.5	73.8	74.8	75.3	77.2	78.0	77.8	77.7	77.0
White, non-Hispanic	83.8	83.6	81.6	83.4	84.3	83.2	82.3	82.7	83.6	83.9	84.3
Black, non-Hispanic	72.7	74.9	73.1	70.0	78.6	63.4	74.6	76.2	67.3	76.1	77.7
Asian, non-Hispanic	74.8	75.3	77.8	73.0	72.5	79.2	78.0	79.1	76.3	73.8	79.2
Rest of USA											
All	82.6	82.2	81.8	81.4	82.2	82.2	82.6	82.7	82.6	83.1	82.8
CalWORKs/TANF/AFDC Status											
Not Enrolled	84.1	83.9	83.4	83.1	83.6	83.4	83.7	83.5	83.2	83.5	83.2
Enrolled	36.2	34.5	35.4	36.1	37.3	39.3	41.5	46.8	50.3	54.8	48.4
Below Poverty Level	49.4	49.3	48.7	48.2	48.9	48.8	49.0	49.5	49.3	51.1	49.0
Race/Ethnicity											
Hispanic	74.9	75.1	74.1	73.4	73.7	73.6	75.2	76.0	76.1	77.4	78.0
White, non-Hispanic	85.0	84.6	84.3	84.1	84.9	85.0	85.2	85.0	84.9	85.1	84.8
Black, non-Hispanic	73.7	73.4	72.5	72.3	73.4	73.4	74.7	76.1	76.4	78.2	77.4
Asian, non-Hispanic	75.6	74.7	76.1	74.1	75.6	76.7	79.2	79.3	78.5	77.0	78.4

Table B.10 Annual Income under Poverty Level

Operational Definition: Percentage of people living in families with income under the federal poverty threshold.

	1990	1991	1992	1993	1994	1995	1996	1997	1998	1999	2000
Los Angeles County											
Countywide	17.4	20.5	21.0	22.8	24.2	23.3	22.0	21.9	19.6	17.1	15.8
CalWORKs/TANF/AFDC Status											
Not Enrolled	14.8	16.7	17.1	18.7	19.1	19.3	18.5	18.1	17.7	14.8	13.5
Enrolled	64.7	76.7	72.6	65.9	76.1	68.0	71.5	78.9	68.1	63.3	65.9
Race/Ethnicity											
Hispanic	28.7	33.0	33.7	35.4	34.9	34.8	31.5	32.3	30.1	25.6	22.0
White, non-Hispanic	7.1	8.9	9.8	9.1	10.9	9.6	11.2	9.2	6.6	7.4	7.9
Black, non-Hispanic	25.6	27.5	25.3	22.3	28.3	26.8	22.7	30.1	20.9	19.7	17.3
Asian, non-Hispanic	8.7	11.6	11.4	18.5	19.9	16.9	18.4	12.2	16.3	10.7	15.3
Rest of California											
All	12.4	13.6	13.5	16.3	15.2	13.9	14.8	14.4	13.7	12.5	11.8
CalWORKs/TANF/AFDC Status											
Not Enrolled	9.3	9.6	9.8	12.8	12.0	10.7	11.2	11.5	11.2	10.9	10.2
Enrolled	58.5	71.2	66.1	65.3	62.9	60.5	76.4	73.1	69.0	56.6	54.0
Race/Ethnicity											
Hispanic	23.9	25.5	23.5	28.6	27.4	24.8	27.8	23.1	22.8	22.3	21.0
White, non-Hispanic	7.6	8.7	9.4	9.7	9.2	7.1	8.9	9.7	9.8	8.3	7.1
Black, non-Hispanic	23.9	19.9	24.2	33.7	19.1	27.6	20.9	21.1	20.0	19.4	13.8
Asian, non-Hispanic	15.2	17.2	12.0	15.8	17.3	17.5	16.2	16.3	10.2	9.0	10.8
Rest of USA											
All	13.4	14.0	14.3	14.9	14.2	13.5	13.4	12.9	12.5	11.6	11.1
CalWORKs/TANF/AFDC Status											
Not Enrolled	10.1	10.5	10.9	11.4	11.2	10.7	10.9	10.8	10.7	10.3	10.1
Enrolled	75.5	77.5	75.8	76.1	73.1	70.6	72.3	75.3	73.5	67.7	65.7
Race/Ethnicity											
Hispanic	27.9	27.9	28.4	29.8	29.9	29.4	29.0	26.2	24.9	22.3	21.1
White, non-Hispanic	8.9	9.4	9.6	9.9	9.4	8.5	8.6	8.6	8.2	7.7	7.5
Black, non-Hispanic	32.0	32.9	33.5	33.2	30.6	29.1	28.3	26.2	26.0	23.7	22.1
Asian, non-Hispanic	12.8	14.2	12.6	14.7	13.9	14.3	13.7	14.0	11.6	10.4	10.3

Table B.11 Percentage of Family Income Used for Housing

Operational Definition: Among all people, the ratio of average family spending on housing to average family income, multiplied by 100.

	1990	1991	1992	1993	1994	1995	1996	1997	1998	1999	2000
Los Angeles County											
Countywide		21.9		24.3		24.1		22.9		20.8	
CalWORKs/TANF/AFDC Status											
Not Enrolled		21.4		23.7		23.3		22.2		20.3	
Enrolled		29.1		34.2		36.1		36.0		30.1	
Below Poverty Level		73.2		79.3		62.8		68.3		71.4	
Race/Ethnicity											
Hispanic		24.6		28.9		27.7		26.4		23.4	
White, non-Hispanic		19.5		21.5		21.4		19.5		18.4	
Black, non-Hispanic		19.6		26.5		22.8		25.3		22.2	
Asian, non-Hispanic		24.6		24.4		25.0		23.9		22.1	
Rest of California											
All		21.1		22.0		22.7		20.7		20.2	
CalWORKs/TANF/AFDC Status											
Not Enrolled		21.0		21.9		22.3		20.3		20.7	
Enrolled		24.2		24.0		37.6		34.2			
Below Poverty Level		76.2		81.4		74.9		68.8		78.3	
Race/Ethnicity											
Hispanic		24.5		25.6		30.3		23.6		19.7	
White, non-Hispanic		20.5		20.8		21.2		19.4		19.8	
Black, non-Hispanic		24.3		24.7		24.9		22.8		22.4	
Asian, non-Hispanic		20.0		23.6		22.3		21.5		21.5	
Rest of USA											
All		17.2		17.5		18.1		17.5		16.6	
CalWORKs/TANF/AFDC Status											
Not Enrolled		16.9		17.3		17.8		17.2		16.4	
Enrolled		26.8		26.5		27.7		27.3		22.7	
Below Poverty Level		48.9		54.2		59.1		63.6		62.9	
Race/Ethnicity											
Hispanic		20.9		21.8		21.9		21.3		19.7	
White, non-Hispanic		16.7		16.9		17.3		16.7		15.7	
Black, non-Hispanic		19.4		20.2		20.4		20.2		20.2	
Asian, non-Hispanic		20.0		20.2		20.5		20.5		19.3	

Table B.12 Personal Behavior Harmful to Self or Others

Operational Definition: Substantiated cases of children abused or neglected per 1,000 children per year.

	1990	1991	1992	1993	1994	1995	1996	1997	1998	1999	2000
Los Angeles County Countywide	31.6	27.0	23.0	28.5	26.9	29.3	37.0	30.0	19.9	17.3	15.7
Rest of California All	18.9	17.0	19.0	14.8	14.7	14.5	13.3	14.8	16.7	13.4	
Rest of USA All	12.7	13.5	14.7	14.8	14.7	14.1	13.7	13.0	12.7	11.5	

Table B.13 Participation in Community Activities

Operational Definition: (1) Percentage of registered voters that voted in the November election; (2) Percentage of voting age population that were registered to vote in the November election; (3) Percentage of voting age population that voted in the November election.

	Percentage of registered voters that voted in the November election			Percentage of the voting-age population that were registered to vote in the November election			Percentage of the voting-age population that voted in the November election		
	1996	1998	2000	1996	1998	2000	1996	1998	2000
Los Angeles County									
Countywide	86.8	78.9	89.0	50.1	47.7	49.5	43.4	37.7	44.0
Race/Ethnicity									
Hispanic	83.1	78.7	88.9	23.6	23.3	29.2	19.6	18.3	25.9
White, non-Hispanic	88.5	80.6	90.0	72.1	69.4	67.1	63.8	55.9	60.4
Black, non-Hispanic	85.3	82.6	87.6	72.8	71.9	66.6	62.1	59.4	58.4
Asian, non-Hispanic	83.4	63.6	85.0	36.1	33.6	38.9	30.1	21.4	33.1
Rest of California									
All	86.2	77.3	87.7	59.2	54.5	54.6	51.1	42.1	47.9
Race/Ethnicity									
Hispanic	76.2	75.3	79.1	32.9	31.3	29.7	25.0	23.6	23.5
White, non-Hispanic	88.0	79.8	90.0	72.1	66.8	67.6	63.4	53.3	60.8
Black, non-Hispanic	85.1	56.3	80.6	61.8	54.1	58.7	52.5	30.5	47.3
Asian, non-Hispanic	83.3	71.0	83.5	30.7	30.8	31.0	25.5	21.9	25.9
Rest of USA									
All	82.1	67.2	85.5	62.6	62.6	64.5	54.6	42.1	55.1
Race/Ethnicity									
Hispanic	74.2	57.5	77.4	35.3	35.3	35.8	27.9	20.3	27.7
White, non-Hispanic	83.1	68.2	86.3	67.9	67.9	70.0	59.5	46.3	60.4
Black, non-Hispanic	79.6	65.1	84.0	60.6	60.6	64.2	50.6	39.4	53.9
Asian, non-Hispanic	78.8	66.2	82.6	28.4	28.5	29.4	25.3	18.9	24.3

Table B.14 Adult Attainment of a High School Diploma or GED

Operational Definition: Percentage of people 18 to 45 who have completed high school or a General Education Degree.

	1990	1991	1992	1993	1994	1995	1996	1997	1998	1999	2000
Los Angeles County											
Countywide	70.2	72.2	73.4	72.9	72.9	72.1	72.9	72.0	72.1	73.7	73.8
CalWORKs/TANF/AFDC Status											
Not Enrolled	70.6	72.8	74.3	74.0	74.2	73.2	74.2	73.3	72.8	74.2	74.6
Enrolled	58.4	52.0	49.0	43.4	44.3	50.4	45.9	38.0	49.9	46.1	40.5
Below Poverty Level	46.1	43.2	44.6	43.7	45.9	48.3	43.9	49.2	48.4	47.3	52.1
Race/Ethnicity											
Hispanic	41.3	44.9	45.5	42.4	46.4	46.5	47.9	43.0	46.2	48.7	48.3
White, non-Hispanic	87.3	87.9	91.2	91.4	90.2	90.5	91.7	92.5	92.2	91.4	92.8
Black, non-Hispanic	81.8	79.6	82.1	80.1	85.4	86.5	81.6	85.6	88.6	88.8	90.2
Asian, non-Hispanic	90.1	87.0	84.8	89.2	87.7	83.9	85.3	86.3	85.0	88.5	84.7
Rest of California											
All	79.1	79.0	80.1	81.0	80.9	80.7	81.0	82.6	82.5	82.2	82.4
CalWORKs/TANF/AFDC Status											
Not Enrolled	79.9	80.0	81.0	81.6	81.9	81.7	81.8	83.4	83.1	82.8	82.8
Enrolled	51.8	49.5	53.5	64.8	56.0	54.4	55.2	57.3	56.0	54.5	57.4
Below Poverty Level	51.2	54.0	56.1	61.2	59.9	54.7	51.0	56.7	62.0	64.5	60.1
Race/Ethnicity											
Hispanic	48.5	45.8	48.3	51.7	51.6	50.5	51.2	55.3	54.3	54.3	55.1
White, non-Hispanic	86.9	88.0	88.9	88.8	90.6	90.8	90.5	90.8	91.6	91.3	91.3
Black, non-Hispanic	80.9	79.8	81.8	85.4	83.6	91.5	83.9	86.6	84.8	86.8	85.8
Asian, non-Hispanic	72.9	76.9	79.0	85.3	85.6	80.8	82.0	85.3	82.9	82.3	87.3
Rest of USA											
All	77.8	78.6	79.4	80.3	80.8	81.4	81.4	81.8	82.5	82.9	83.4
CalWORKs/TANF/AFDC Status											
Not Enrolled	78.5	79.3	80.2	80.9	81.5	82.0	81.9	82.3	82.9	83.2	83.7
Enrolled	51.9	52.7	54.3	58.2	60.0	60.7	60.3	60.3	59.5	61.6	57.6
Below Poverty Level	50.0	52.1	53.1	55.9	57.1	57.3	56.9	58.1	59.0	61.3	61.3
Race/Ethnicity											
Hispanic	53.4	53.1	54.7	55.4	55.5	54.8	55.2	56.7	57.3	57.8	58.2
White, non-Hispanic	81.4	82.4	83.2	83.9	84.6	85.4	85.4	85.7	86.5	86.9	87.6
Black, non-Hispanic	66.5	67.2	67.7	70.5	72.6	73.1	73.7	74.5	75.6	76.3	77.3
Asian, non-Hispanic	79.0	80.6	83.0	83.4	84.8	83.6	83.5	84.7	85.6	84.5	85.5

Table B.15 Elementary and Secondary School Students Reading at Grade Level

Operational Definition: Percentage of elementary and secondary students (third and ninth grade) performing at or above median for grade in the California Standardized Testing and Reporting program.

Third Grade Level	1990	1991	1992	1993	1994	1995	1996	1997	1998	1999	2000
Los Angeles County											
Countywide									29.0	31.0	34.0
Race/Ethnicity											
Hispanic									15.0	17.0	21.0
White, non-Hispanic									59.0	63.0	67.0
Black, non-Hispanic									22.0	26.0	30.0
Asian, non-Hispanic									53.0	57.0	62.0
Rest of California											
All									41.0	45.0	48.0
Race/Ethnicity											
Hispanic									18.0	22.0	26.0
White, non-Hispanic									59.0	64.0	68.0
Black, non-Hispanic									25.0	31.0	35.0
Asian, non-Hispanic									45.0	50.0	54.0

Ninth Grade Level	1990	1991	1992	1993	1994	1995	1996	1997	1998	1999	2000
Los Angeles County											
Countywide									26.0	26.0	27.0
Race/Ethnicity											
Hispanic									13.0	14.0	15.0
White, non-Hispanic									52.0	51.0	53.0
Black, non-Hispanic									17.0	19.0	19.0
Asian, non-Hispanic									48.0	48.0	51.0
Rest of California											
All									37.0	37.0	38.0
Race/Ethnicity											
Hispanic									16.0	16.0	17.0
White, non-Hispanic									53.0	53.0	54.0
Black, non-Hispanic									20.0	21.0	21.0
Asian, non-Hispanic									40.0	41.0	43.0

Table B.16 Teenage High School Graduation

Operational Definition: Ratio of the number of high school graduates to the number of students entering ninth grade three academic years previous.

	1990	1991	1992	1993	1994	1995	1996	1997	1998	1999	2000
Los Angeles County											
Countywide								62.3	62.5	62.5	62.4
Race/Ethnicity											
Hispanic								52.5	53.1	53.1	52.4
White, non-Hispanic								74.5	73.9	76.7	77.4
Black, non-Hispanic								56.0	54.6	54.0	56.8
Asian, non-Hispanic								90.3	92.7	89.9	90.1
Rest of California											
All								67.7	68.9	70.3	70.8
Race/Ethnicity											
Hispanic								55.5	56.7	58.9	59.7
White, non-Hispanic								73.6	75.0	76.7	77.6
Black, non-Hispanic								55.0	56.4	58.4	58.5
Asian, non-Hispanic								85.2	86.9	84.1	83.9
USA											
All								67.6	67.7	67.1	67.0

Table B.17 Mother's Educational Attainment at Child's Birth

Operational Definition: Average years of education among women giving birth in each year.

	1990	1991	1992	1993	1994	1995	1996	1997	1998	1999	2000
Los Angeles County											
Countywide		11.0	11.0	11.1	11.1	11.2	11.3	11.5	11.6	11.7	
Race/Ethnicity											
Hispanic		9.2	9.3	9.5	9.6	9.7	9.8	10.0	10.2	10.3	
White, non-Hispanic		13.7	13.8	13.9	13.9	14.0	14.0	14.2	14.2	14.4	
Black, non-Hispanic		12.6	12.6	12.6	12.6	12.6	12.7	12.8	12.8	12.9	
Asian, non-Hispanic		13.4	13.4	13.5	13.5	13.6	13.8	13.9	14.0	14.1	
Supervisory Districts											
SD-1		9.8	9.8	9.9	10.0	10.1	10.2	10.3	10.4	10.6	
SD-2		10.1	10.1	10.1	10.2	10.3	10.4	10.6	10.7	10.8	
SD-3		11.3	11.4	11.5	11.5	11.6	11.6	11.9	12.0	12.1	
SD-4		11.9	11.9	11.9	12.0	12.0	12.1	12.3	12.4	12.4	
SD-5		12.7	12.7	12.7	12.8	12.8	12.8	13.0	13.0	13.1	
Service Planning Areas											
Antelope Valley (1)		12.2	12.2	12.2	12.2	12.1	12.0	12.0	12.0	12.1	
San Fernando Valley (2)		11.6	11.6	11.7	11.8	11.8	11.9	12.0	12.1	12.2	
San Gabriel Valley (3)		11.5	11.5	11.6	11.6	11.7	11.7	11.9	12.0	12.1	
Metro (4)		9.8	9.8	9.9	10.0	10.2	10.2	10.4	10.5	10.8	
West (5)		13.7	13.6	13.6	13.6	13.8	13.8	14.0	14.2	14.3	
South (6)		9.5	9.5	9.6	9.6	9.7	9.8	9.9	10.0	10.1	
East (7)		10.6	10.7	10.8	10.8	10.9	10.9	11.1	11.2	11.3	
South Bay (8)		11.5	11.6	11.6	11.7	11.7	11.8	12.0	12.1	12.1	
Rest of California											
All		11.8	11.8	11.9	11.8	12.0	12.1	12.2	12.3	12.3	
Race/Ethnicity											
Hispanic		9.7	9.7	9.8	9.9	10.1	10.1	10.3	10.4	10.5	
White, non-Hispanic		13.3	13.4	13.5	13.5	13.6	13.7	13.7	13.8	13.9	
Black, non-Hispanic		12.4	12.5	12.5	12.4	12.5	12.6	12.6	12.7	12.7	
Asian, non-Hispanic		11.8	12	12.4	12.4	12.6	13	13.3	13.6	13.7	

Table B.18 Adult Participation in Education or Vocational Training
Operational Definition: Percent of people 18–45 who are enrolled in education or vocational training.

	1990	1991	1992	1993	1994	1995	1996	1997	1998	1999	2000
Los Angeles County											
Countywide		17.0	15.3	15.9	16.3	14.4	18.3	18.2	17.7	17.7	
Race/Ethnicity											
Hispanic		13.3	11.4	11.9	13.0	12.0	15.0	13.7	14.7	13.6	
White, non-Hispanic		17.5	15.9	17.3	17.9	14.9	19.7	19.6	20.5	18.5	
Black, non-Hispanic		21.0	17.7	18.2	16.0	21.6	19.1	23.4	19.6	19.8	
Asian, non-Hispanic		27.7	27.6	23.1	24.8	20.2	25.7	26.6	20.2	30.0	
Rest of California											
All		18.2	16.5	16.7	16.5	16.8	18.2	19.7	18.5	17.8	
Race/Ethnicity											
Hispanic		12.1	12.6	13.5	13.7	11.4	11.6	12.5	12.7	11.7	
White, non-Hispanic		19.1	16.6	16.6	17.0	18.2	19.9	20.7	19.2	18.9	
Black, non-Hispanic		16.9	16.2	23.1	18.4	19.4	22.9	26.0	20.8	17.9	
Asian, non-Hispanic		27.1	25.8	23.4	21.1	22.6	21.5	25.1	25.8	25.3	
Rest of USA											
All		15.8	15.9	16.0	16.1	16.0	16.0	16.1	16.4	15.8	
Race/Ethnicity											
Hispanic		12.2	13.2	13.9	13.7	13.3	12.7	12.4	12.9	12.4	
White, non-Hispanic		15.9	16.0	16.0	16.1	16.2	16.0	16.3	16.4	15.9	
Black, non-Hispanic		14.9	15.0	15.5	15.8	15.8	16.4	15.8	17.2	16.4	
Asian, non-Hispanic		26.5	24.9	25.6	25.6	24.4	23.3	23.5	23.9	22.6	

REFERENCES

Burbridge, L.C., and D.S. Nightingale, *Local Coordination of Employment and Training Services to Welfare Recipients*, Washington, D.C.: The Urban Institute, 1989.

Burt, Martha R., Laudan Y. Aron, Toby Douglas, Jesse Valente, Edgar Lee and Britta Iwen, *Homelessness: Programs And The People They Serve. Findings of the National Survey of Homeless Assistance Providers and Clients,* Washington, D.C.: The Urban Institute, December 1999.

Davis, Lois M., Jacob Alex Klerman, Elaine Reardon, Sarah C. Remes, and Paul S. Steinberg, *Countywide Evaluation of the Long-Term Family Self-Sufficiency Plan: Assessing the Utility of the LTFSS Plan Service Delivery and Planning Framework*, Santa Monica, CA: RAND, DRU-2700-12-LTFSSP, 2001.

Friedman, Mark, *Results and Performance Accountability Implementation Guide*, Fiscal Policy Studies Institute, http://www.raguide.org/, 2001.

Greenfeld, L.A., M.R. Rand, D. Craven, P.A. Klaus, C.A. Perkins, C. Ringel, G. Warchol, C. Maston, and J. A. Fox, *Violence Against Intimates: Analysis of Data on Crimes by Current or Former Spouses, Boyfriends, and Girlfriends*, Washington, D.C.: Bureau of Justice Statistics, U.S. Department of Justice, 1998.

Hack, M., N.K. Klein, and H.G. Taylor, "Long-Term Developmental Outcomes of Low Birth Weight," *The Future of Children: Low Birth Weight,* 5(1):176–196, Los Altos, CA: Center for the Future of Children, The David and Lucile Packard Foundation, 1995.

Hedderson, John, and Robert F. Schoeni, *LTFSS Plan Countywide Evaluation: Indicators, Data Sources, and Geographical Units of Analysis*, Santa Monica, CA: RAND, DRU-2797-LTFSSP, July 2001.

Holcomb, P.A., K.S. Seefeldt, J. Trutko, B.S. Barnow, and D.S. Nightingale, *One Stop Shopping Service Integration: Major Dimensions, Key Characteristics and Impediments to Implementation*, Washington, D.C.: The Urban Institute, 1993.

Klerman, Jacob Alex, Gail L. Zellman, Tammi Chun, Nicole Humphrey, Elaine Reardon, Donna O. Farley, Patricia A. Ebener, and Paul S. Steinberg, *Welfare Reform in California: State and County Implementation of CalWORKs in the Second Year,* Santa Monica, CA: RAND, MR-1177-CDSS, 2000

Lewit, E.M., L.S. Baker, H. Corman, and P.H. Shiono, "The Direct Cost of Low Birth Weight," *The Future of Children: Low Birth Weight, 5*(1):87–102, Los Altos, CA: Center for the Future of Children, The David and Lucile Packard Foundation, 1995.

Liner, B., H.P. Hatry, E. Vinson, R. Allen, P. Dusenbury, and S. Bryant, "Making Results-Based Government Work," Washington, D.C.: The Urban Institute, 2001.

Los Angeles County, *Long-Term Family Self-Sufficiency Plan Evaluation Design*, October 23, 2000.

Los Angeles County Children's Planning Council, *Laying the Groundwork for Change: Los Angeles County's First Action Plan for Its Children, Youth and Families,* January 1998.

Los Angeles County Children's Planning Council, *Profiles of Los Angeles County Service Planning Area Resources for Children, Youth, and Families*, May 1996.

Los Angeles County Children's Planning Council and United Way of Greater Los Angeles, *Los Angeles County Children's Scorecard 1998*, January 1999.

Los Angeles Department of Public Social Services, http://dpss.co.la.ca.us/urd/chart_six.cfm (accessed 8/6/01).

Martinson, Karin, *Literature Review on Service Coordination and Integration in the Welfare and Workforce Development Systems*, Washington, D.C.: The Urban Institute, 1999.

Morley, E., E. Vinson, and H.P. Hatry, *Outcome Measurement in Nonprofit Organizations: Current Practices and Recommendations*, Independent Sector and The Urban Institute, 2001.

New Directions Task Force, *Long-Term Family Self-Sufficiency Plan,* County of Los Angeles, October 1999.

Paneth, N.S., "The Problem of Low Birth Weight," *The Future of Children: Low Birth Weight, 5*(1)19–34, Los Altos, CA: Center for the Future of Children, The David and Lucile Packard Foundation, 1995.

Rennison, C.M., *Intimate Partner Violence,* Washington, D.C.: Bureau of Justice Statistics, U.S. Department of Justice, 2000.

Rossi, Peter H., Howard E. Freeman, and Mark W. Lipsey, *Evaluation: A Systematic Approach*, sixth edition, Thousand Oaks, CA: Sage Publications, 1999.

Schoeni, Robert F., Jeanne Ringel, John Hedderson, Paul S. Steinberg, Laura Hickman, Eric Eide, Marian Bussey, and John Fluke, *Countywide Evaluation of the Long-Term Family Self-Sufficiency Plan: Establishing the Baselines*, Santa Monica, CA: RAND, MR-1466-LTFSS, 2001.

Trutko, J., L. Bailis, B. Barnow, and S. French, *An Assessment of the JTPA Role In State And Local Coordination Activities*, Washington, D.C.: U.S. Department of Labor Employment and Training Administration, 1991.